**DO NOT REMOVE
CARDS FROM POCKET**

A Dawn in the Trees

A Dawn
in the Trees

Thomas Jefferson, the Years 1776 to 1789

LEONARD WIBBERLEY

Ariel Books · Farrar, Straus and Company · New York

A Dawn in the Trees

☆

1

The task of writing was done. It had taken seventeen days during which time Thomas Jefferson, delegate from Virginia in the Third Continental Congress, had sat for hours alone in a rented room on the second floor of a bricklayer's house at the corner of Market and Seventh streets in Philadelphia, drawing up the document which he had been assigned to produce by a committee of the Congress.

He wrote on a portable writing desk made to his order by a Philadelphia carpenter. He was delighted with this desk for he loved to write and had often in the past during his travels been unable to find even a table to write on. The desk, containing paper, quill pens, ink and sandbox, folded up into a small package which could be carried by hand or on horseback, so that never in the future would Tom Jefferson be without the tools of a writer.

While he had been at work, Jefferson begged his friends to leave him alone. Business he was prepared to discuss with them. But he did not want any social calls for he hated to be interrupted while he was writing. Mrs. Graff, his landlord's wife, worried about him. He got up at dawn every day, poured water from a large jug into a basin and then bathed his feet in the water which was frigid from standing all night in the jug.

Such a procedure would surely produce a shocking cold. Then, at six in the morning and again at noon, he religiously inspected a thermometer which he had hung in the shade outside the house and made a note of the temperature. Her lodger was devoted to this thermometer which was one of the first things he had bought on arrival in Philadelphia. He had paid a monstrous sum for it—several pounds. And what did it do? Well, it told you whether it was hot or cold, which any sensible person could discover for himself by putting his head out of the door.

He was a very polite man and no trouble at all around the house, and Mrs. Graff sometimes thought that he was interested in setting up a bricklaying business, for he plied her husband with questions about his trade. Not many gentlemen bothered to talk to bricklayers and other artisans, but Mr. Thomas Jefferson seemed fascinated by them. He wanted to know how many bricks of a standard size a bricklayer could lay in an hour, how long the bricks should be soaked in water before being laid, whether pure water was best for soaking the bricks in or whether dirty water was just as good.

"He's a very odd gentleman indeed, Mr. Graff," the bricklayer's wife said to her husband one evening. "Bathes his feet every morning, looks at that thing outside to see how hot it is, writes all day and asks questions when he isn't writing. He wanted to know today how much a yard I paid for a fine homespun, and what was the earliest day each year strawberries could be had from the fruiters in the town."

"He's one of the quality," said the bricklayer. "They're all a bit odd. Maybe he's writing something about laying bricks," he added.

"Or running a household," said his wife. "Young girls these days don't know much about it, I'll warrant you. Why my mother . . ." But Mr. Graff didn't listen to the rest. It seemed that everybody's mother was a genius when it came to running a house.

The document on which Tom Jefferson had been working from June 11 to June 28, 1776, was the Declaration of Independence. He hadn't asked for the task. It had been wished on him by a committee formed to produce such a Declaration. The committee agreed upon the principles and turned the job over to Jefferson. Jefferson was a modest man, taking no pride at all in his own talents, and he suggested that John Adams of Massachusetts should write the Declaration, urging that Adams was far better known than he and also better equipped for the job.

But Adams would have none of it. "Mr. Jefferson,"

★

5

he said, "I will give you two good reasons why I should not write this Declaration. First, I am not altogether popular with the Congress. Second, you are a far better writer than I."

So Jefferson took to his room and now the work was done. Not only was it done, but he had recopied the whole thing so as to have a fairly legible copy to show to his committee. He took it first to the two members of the committee he held in the highest esteem, Benjamin Franklin and John Adams.

"Please make whatever alterations you think necessary," he said. "Don't hold back for fear of hurting my feelings. The Declaration is more important than I. It must be sound. It must say exactly what we want, and plainly so that the world will understand why we are taking this position."

Franklin, the Declaration in his hand, peered over the top of his steel-rimmed spectacles at Jefferson. "Do you think that you have put anything into it that is original—that comes entirely from yourself? Some new principle of government which we had not thought of?"

"No," said Jefferson. "I have not attempted anything new but have only stated those principles of freedom recognized as the proper rights of man by all who have thought and written on the subject. I have tried to bring all together in one statement, made clearly and without quibbling, believing, as I know you believe, that truth alone has any lasting value."

★
6

"And on slavery?"

"You know my stand on slavery. I abhor it. So do you. I have denounced it. It should be denounced. It should be abolished. How can we establish a nation of free men, ourselves supporting slavery?"

Franklin nodded and seemed for some moments to be in deep thought. He himself came from poor circumstances and had never owned a slave. Jefferson came of the landed gentlemen of Virginia and owned several hundred. Yet Jefferson was vehemently opposed to slavery and retained his slaves because if he set them free they would starve and if he paid them he would be unable to compete with other slave owners who paid no wages.

"Mr. Jefferson," Franklin said, "we must stand before we can walk; walk before we can run; run before we can ride; ride before we can fly." He considered the prospect of men flying for a moment. The words had come unbidden. Was it possible that men would one day fly, or was he talking nonsense? Perhaps some key to the question lay in the weight of the bones of birds as opposed to the bones of men. He should get the skeleton of a large bird and weigh the bones carefully and equate their weight if the bird were the size of a man. His mind wandered on and Jefferson waited patiently.

"The question of slavery," Jefferson said at length, prompting him.

"Ah yes," said Franklin. "There may be trouble there.

★

7

Too many interests are involved—north and south. I will support you. But we must not hazard all on this one question alone."

They dined together that night and frequently in the days that followed, but talked little of the Declaration. Jefferson, the task done, seemed to have put it out of his mind since it was no longer in his hands. Actually Franklin, Adams and the other members of the committee made very few changes in the draft Declaration as Jefferson had set it down. Of the members of the committee, John Adams was the most outspoken.

"I will fight for the Declaration until the last dog is hung—and I will hang him myself, sir," he told Jefferson. "The northern colonies are with us. You have nothing to fear from New England. They're as solid as a wall. Virginia, we know, is for independence, and the southern colonies are ripening to the thought. But the middle colonies—there's the trouble. I tell you that fellow Dickinson has made but one firm decision in his life and that was never to make any decisions at all. He has spent his life reducing 'yes' to 'perhaps' and 'no' to 'maybe' and in that kind of work he has a genius all his own."

John Dickinson was the leader of the Pennsylvania delegation to the Continental Congress and even at this late date clung to the pathetic hope that the colonies could be reconciled to the Mother Country, England.

"It is my opinion that he will be persuaded to join us," said Jefferson.

★
8

"It is my opinion that when the vote is taken, he won't be there," snapped Adams.

Actually the Declaration of Independence had been drawn up in anticipation of the Continental Congress's passing a far more important measure. This was a resolution, presented to the Congress by Richard Henry Lee of Virginia, boldly stating that the colonies ought to be free of Great Britain and establish themselves as a self-governing nation.

"Resolved that these United Colonies are, and of right ought to be, free and independent States, that they are absolved from all allegiance to the British Crown, and that all political connection between them and the State of Great Britain is and ought to be totally dissolved."

Those were the words of the Virginia Resolution, proposed to the Congress on June 7. They were received with cheers by some and dismay by others. A long debate followed, lasting two days, and then it was proposed to put off any vote on the resolution until July 1, by which time delegates would have had time to consult with their own legislatures and make up their minds how to vote.

So the most important business immediately before the Congress was not Thomas Jefferson's Declaration of Independence, but Richard Henry Lee's resolution calling for independence. Once that was passed—if it were passed—then the Declaration itself, which would formalize the decision for the benefit of the world, would be considered.

★

The debate on the Virginia Resolution calling for independence opened early on July 1, in Carpenters Hall, Philadelphia, where the meetings of the Continental Congress were held.

Thomas Jefferson had been up at dawn, as usual, had bathed his feet, as usual, and had recorded the temperature at six in the morning, as usual.

Though he wrote well he was no orator, for his voice in public speaking was high-pitched and his meticulous mind did not allow him the flights of fancy, the appeals to the emotions, the scorn and irony and humor that made Patrick Henry the most famous orator of the day. He had determined not to speak on the Virginia Resolution for other reasons. He was himself a delegate from Virginia. It was plain then that he supported the resolution. Support from colonies other than Virginia was what was needed. Jefferson hoped to get that support from John Adams. He hoped that Adams would second and speak strongly for its adoption.

An alliance between Virginia and Massachusetts which Adams represented would demonstrate the unity of the colonies to those who were inclined to think, though secretly, that the quarrel with Britain was primarily a quarrel between the New England states and the Crown. That sentiment was not often voiced, but it lay hidden in the private thinking of some of the delegates. After all, what injury had England ever inflicted on Delaware, or Maryland, or Pennsylvania?

Jefferson was deeply attached to John Adams. He

loved the honesty of his mind, his liberality of view, his courage in stating his convictions, his ability to get to the heart of matters and not get bogged down in details.

Adams rose to the occasion. When the Virginia Resolution was submitted to the Congress, it was Adams who seconded the resolution and Adams who beat down all the opposition. But the opposition was formidable and came principally from John Dickinson, leader of the big Pennsylvania delegation.

Dickinson was very highly respected. He had so often written of the rights of the colonies in their quarrel with England, which he called the Mother Country, that he was called the "Penman of the Revolution." To him had often fallen the task of drafting petitions for the redress of the grievances of the colonies addressed to the British Parliament, to the people of England and to the King of England.

His prose was elegant and his appearance was as elegant as his prose. His wig was well powdered and combed. He wore sober dark clothing, usually black, to which his snow white linen presented a fetching contrast. He spoke with fire and conviction against a formal Declaration of Independence and said that he knew that what he was about to say would cost him his reputation. But his conscience demanded that regardless of his reputation, he speak out for what he believed. The decision the Congress faced had never before been taken by Britons or the descendants of Britons—the decision to cut themselves off forever

★

11

from the land of their fathers, from its laws, its commerce, its government, its traditions and its protection.

Here was a terrible leap to be made into the dark and Dickinson warned eloquently against it. The delegates should not, he said, take so great a step without that step being demanded of them by the people they represented. Such a demand had not come from the people so far. Many of the colonies were not prepared to vote for independence. If some voted for it and others against it, there would be a split among the colonies. The dissenters might secede from the proposed union and nothing but discord would result. Furthermore, while some argued that France and Spain would welcome an American Declaration of Independence and would then give aid to the American cause, that might not be the case. France might be alarmed at the rise of a new power on the North American continent. Britain might secretly ally herself with France to bring about the ruin of the new American nation. Independence, he warned, could mean only outright war. The colonies were not in any condition to fight so great a power as England and had no allies. "What you ask," he said, "is that we burn down our house in mid-winter and have no other house to shelter us."

So the arguments went, presented by Dickinson with great sincerity, and they had a marked effect on the delegates.

He spoke at length, quoting often from his own

writings on the subject of independence and when he had done nobody rose immediately to reply to him.

A nervous silence settled over the assembly, interrupted only by the buzzing of the innumerable horseflies that infested the hall, which came from a livery stable next door. The delegates eyed each other, waiting for someone to rise and speak and soon they were all looking at Tom Jefferson, sitting a head higher than the rest of them.

Jefferson did not look up, but continued making notes of what Dickinson had said. Then, when it seemed that no answer was to be given, stocky John Adams rose, his jowl set like a bulldog's, and beat down point by point the whole of Dickinson's objection.

What was all the learned quibbling about? he demanded. The resolution before the Congress would only acknowledge a fact that already existed. They had established their independence by opposing the King's Redcoats and to talk of waiting to hear from the people was nonsense. They had heard from the people in musket shot at Bunker Hill and elsewhere. The King himself had made the colonies independent by declaring them out of his protection and levying war against them. If Pennsylvania and Maryland were holding back, maybe the reason was that they hadn't been attacked by the enemy. . . .

John Adams had a gift for sarcasm and he used it to effect saying that, as far as Pennsylvania was concerned, it was not a case of the delegates being ahead

★

of the people but the people being ahead of the delegates.

"In Pennsylvania we have seen at times a curious
contradiction—nonrepresentative representatives," he
said.

The thrust went home for Pennsylvania had little
or no representation for her frontiersmen and small
farmers who, a few years previously, had been so angered at their government that they had marched on
Philadelphia armed with rifles. All the persuasiveness
of Benjamin Franklin had been required to prevent
them from entering and perhaps looting the City of
Brotherly Love.

When Adams had done, a vote on the Virginia Resolution calling for a break with Britain was taken. Voting for the break were New Hampshire, Connecticut,
Massachusetts, Rhode Island, New Jersey, Maryland,
Virginia, North Carolina and Georgia. South Carolina
and Pennsylvania voted against it. Delaware had only
two members present and they were divided. New
York abstained from voting until new instructions were
received.

Nine of the colonies then were for independence,
two were against it and two abstained. At this point
Mr. Edward Rutledge of South Carolina requested
that the decision be put off to the next day. "At that
time," he said, "it is possible that my delegation will
vote for the resolution for the sake of unanimity."

"We have wasted the whole day in infernal prattle,"
said John Adams to Jefferson as they left the hall.

"There was not one single word said in the whole of nine hours that had not been said a hundred times before in the past six months."

"The day was not wasted," said Jefferson quietly. "Tomorrow South Carolina, I am persuaded, will vote for the resolution and then we will have ten for and one against. Caesar Rodney is expected at any moment from Delaware. If he is here by tomorrow, that will break the deadlock there. They are caught in a tide, sir, and protest as they will, they cannot resist it."

But John Adams would not be comforted. New England born and bred, he liked matters plainly put and went off grumbling about Philadelphia and lawyers (for Dickinson was, among other things, a lawyer). "Philadelphia lawyers," he snorted in disgust, coining a phrase without being aware of it. He was so angry that after supper he sat up and wrote a letter by candlelight to a friend, complaining that the whole day had been wasted rehashing arguments that had been hackneyed weeks before.

It was perhaps George Washington who unwittingly produced a unanimous vote for independence when the Congress met again the following day, July 2.

Hardly had the members taken their places when a dispatch rider flung in from Washington's headquarters in New York. He had ridden day and night —and ridden hard—for the news he carried was both grave and urgent. Mr. Benjamin Harrison, temporary president of the Congress, opened the letter the dispatch rider handed to him and read it to the members.

★
15

British warships were massing in huge numbers off New York. An attack on the city was imminent and Washington said that with the small army at his command every exertion would be needed to prevent a major disaster. He needed men, materials and support quickly.

That settled the matter for South Carolina. The colony changed its vote from "No" to "Yes," supporting the resolution for independence. A change had taken place in the voting of the Pennsylvania delegation. John Dickinson was absent. He could not and would not vote for independence. Ben Franklin was present and seated right next to Jefferson. The Pennsylvania delegation changed its vote to one in favor of independence.

The count was now eleven for independence with only Delaware and New York unheard from. During the night, one of lashing rains and thunderstorms, Caesar Rodney of the Delaware delegation had arrived mud-splattered and weary. He had ridden eighty miles to cast his vote and the Delaware delegation, previously divided, now also voted for independence.

Only New York refrained from voting, awaiting fresh instructions. But in the light of the news from Washington, there was no doubt which way New York would vote.

The resolution was passed. There was no turning back now. Independence had been formally voted by the Congress representing the colonies.

"Well, sir," said Franklin, turning to Jefferson after

★

the vote was taken, "we have now only your Declaration ahead of us. May I give you some advice?"

"I would be glad of it," said Jefferson.

"While they are going over your Declaration," said the wise Franklin, "you will suffer less if you think of it as having been written by someone else."

2

The debate in the Congress on the Declaration of Independence was perhaps the greatest ordeal of Tom Jefferson's public life to that time. Once the resolution for independence had passed, the delegates turned to the Declaration over which Jefferson had labored for days in the loneliness of his room in the bricklayer's house.

They went over his draft word by word, sentence by sentence, paragraph by paragraph. At times they haggled for an hour or more over a single word, while Jefferson writhed in his seat, fighting back his natural inclination to defend the document. But he had determined to say not a word on his own behalf, leaving its defense to John Adams and others of his friends.

Two changes in the Declaration irritated him especially. The first was his charge that the British people shared with the King the responsibility for the ill treatment of the American colonies which had driven them to rebellion. From Jefferson's point of view, the people of Great Britain could, through their elected representatives in the Parliament, have prevented the abuses heaped on Americans by the King and his ministers. They had not done so, but had continually returned to office members of Parliament who had supported the King's abuses in the past.

This whole charge against the British people was greatly watered down by the Congress and Jefferson regarded this as contemptible.

Let the facts be plainly stated and the responsibility put where it belonged. That was his point of view. But the Congress felt that there were still many in Britain who sympathized with the American cause, and it would be folly to alienate these with a blanket charge against the whole people of the country.

Jefferson was hardly just in putting so much blame on the British people. Great Britain at this time had a population of about eight million. But so outdated was the election system that eleven thousand voters in key cities elected 257 members of Parliament—more than half the membership of the House of Commons. Prosperous cities such as Manchester and Birmingham could not elect a single member to Parliament, while hamlets such as Old Sarum, built around a fort erected by the Romans, elected seven. In fact, Old Sarum had more members of Parliament than constituents entitled to vote. In fifty-one constituencies there were less than

★

fifty voters. In some only one man had the right to vote. His single ballot elected a member to Parliament and he sold his vote to the highest bidder. Indeed, while the Declaration of Independence was being debated in Philadelphia, John Wilkes in England was working to reform the whole system of electing a Parliament in England.

But Jefferson did not know this and he was blind to the impotence of the British voter. He had never been to England at this time and could not guess at the corruption of the whole system of government there; he tended to think of Englishmen as having the same vigor and freedom of expression as Americans. He said nothing while his charge against the whole people of Britain was watered down. But he never forgot that change. It rankled with him years later, and he described it as pusillanimous.

The second change which angered Jefferson was one which Franklin had warned him to expect. In his charges against King George III, he included the following:

"He (King George III) has waged cruel war against human nature itself, violating its most sacred rights of life and liberty in the persons of a distant people who never offended him, captivating and carrying them into slavery in another hemisphere, or to incur miserable death in their transportation hither. This piratical warfare, the opprobrium of infidel powers, is the warfare of the Christian King of Great Britain. Determined to keep open a market where men should be

★

bought and sold, he has prostituted his negative for suppressing every legislative attempt to prohibit or restrain this execrable commerce. And that this assemblage of horrors might want no fact of distinguished die, he is now exciting these very people to rise in arms among us, and to purchase that liberty of which he has deprived them, by murdering the people on whom he also obtruded them; thus paying off former crimes committed against the liberties of one people, with crimes which he urges them to commit against the lives of another."

The language is out of date but the sense still comes strongly true. Jefferson held King George responsible for the continuance of the slave trade. Jefferson had always been horrified by slavery. He could not countenance the selling of human beings like so many animals. He maintained that slavery destroyed the character of the slave owner, who could vent his anger unbridled on a slave whenever he wanted, and could teach his children by example to do the same. It was true that King George had "prostituted his negative," that is, he abused his power of veto to block any legislation to abolish the slave trade or even reduce the terrible punishments to which slaves were subjected for the slightest resistance to bondage.

But King George had many supporters in his stand, a great number of them in the American colonies. The delegates of South Carolina and Georgia would have none of Jefferson's indictment of slavery. Both these colonies were strongly opposed to any attempt to reduce the slave trade, for slaves were widely used on the plantations there. And the northern colonies profited from the slave trade too, for it was they who sent the ships to Africa to obtain slaves, sold at a handsome profit to the southerners.

Rhode Island at one time had as many as 150 ships a year engaged in the slave trade. So the clause denouncing slavery was stricken out of the Declaration of Independence, and Jefferson remarked to Franklin that whatever the Congress did, the matter of slavery would one day come to a terrible climax in the United States.

"I hope I am not alive when that climax comes," he said.

Franklin made no reply.

The debate on the Declaration of Independence extended from July 2 to July 4. Jefferson's anguish was such that it was evident on his features and Franklin, knowing what he was going through, comforted him.

"I have always made it a rule," he said, "never to draft any kind of paper that is to be the subject of public debate. The pain is as much as may be borne. I am reminded of a hatter who made that mistake and who suffered much of what you are enduring now."

"A hatter?" asked Jefferson, surprised.

"Yes, sir," said Franklin. "A hatter, a good sincere man who wanted to get everything right. He composed a sign that read 'John Thompson, Hatter, Makes and Sells Hats for ready money,' with a picture of a hat underneath the wording. He then took the sign to his friends and asked them what they thought of it. One said it was a good sign but the word 'hatter' was not needed. It was obvious that a hatter made hats, so the word could be dropped. The hatter agreed and removed the word. Another friend questioned the phrase 'for ready money.' What else would a man sell hats for but ready money? Those words went too and the sign became 'John Thompson Makes and Sells Hats,' with the picture of a hat underneath.

" 'Why put in "makes hats"?' asked another friend. 'Plainly you are a hatter and plainly you make hats so that should go out.' These words were removed. A last friend counseled the removal of the words 'sells hats.' 'If you are a hatter,' he said, 'it is obvious to the whole world that you sell hats.' The final sign," Franklin concluded, "contained merely the words 'John Thompson' with a picture of a hat underneath. That's what comes of submitting something you have written to a committee, even of your friends."

Jefferson chuckled, his heart warmed even more to Benjamin Franklin whom he already held in deep affection. The past few years had been extremely hard for the seventy-year-old Franklin. Only three years previously his wife had died and he missed her sorely. He was estranged from his son William, who was loyal to Britain and indeed the royal governor of New Jersey. His whole private life had been shattered in his old age and his public life was shattered too, for Franklin had dreamed of an America which remained in the British Empire and was given room to grow

★

there. That dream had proved hopeless. He had worked hard to achieve it, and he had been deceived and betrayed by the blindness of the British ministers and the British King.

Tom Jefferson knew that it had cost Ben Franklin a terrible searching of his soul to turn his back on Britain and come out for independence, using his enormous influence to persuade the Philadelphia delegation to make the break with England. And yet here was Franklin sitting beside him, despite all his own troubles, public and private, trying to soften for him the ordeal of the public debate on his draft of the Declaration of Independence.

Jefferson was not a demonstrative man. He knew intensities of grief and of love but he suffered these always alone and did not like to make any show of his emotions. But when Franklin had told him the story of the hatter, he reached out and touched the withering hand of the old statesman and philosopher and said gently, "Thank you, Doctor Franklin."

Others came to the defense of Jefferson's words and always foremost among them was John Adams. Both Jefferson and Adams wanted to abolish forever the word "colonies" and substitute for it the word "states" in any reference to the different provinces of America. All through the draft of the Declaration, Jefferson had substituted, wherever possible, the word "states" for "colonies" and he was frustrated to find the Congress reversing this change.

In the critical paragraph of the Declaration he had

★

24

written, "We, therefore, the representatives of the United States of America in General Congress assembled, appealing to the Supreme Judge of the world for the rectitude of our intentions, do in the name, and by the authority of the good people of these *states*, reject and renounce all allegiance and subjection to the kings of Great Britain. . . ."

Congress changed this to read, ". . . do in the name and by the authority of the good people of these *Colonies*, solemnly publish and declare, that these united *Colonies* are, and of right ought to be free and independent States; that they are absolved from all allegiance to the British crown. . . ."

The point at issue was that, until the Declaration was official, the states were colonies and that point of view was perhaps legally correct. But Jefferson maintained that the King and his ministers had themselves cut off the American people from Britain, and thus even before the Declaration the different American provinces had ceased to be British colonies.

The debate continued until the evening of Thursday, the Fourth of July. When all were in agreement, it was read through with all the changes—the first public reading of the Declaration of Independence as we know it now. It was listened to in profound silence. None of the rolling power of Jefferson's language had been destroyed. It marched clause by clause to its final noble climax, concluding with Jefferson's unaltered words, "And, for the support of this Declaration, with a firm reliance on the protection of Divine Providence, we mutually pledge to each other our lives, our fortunes, and our sacred honor."

When the last word was uttered, not a sound was heard in the assembly room. It was late evening and the street noises had died away—the rumbling of coach and wagon wheels and the cracking of the carters' whips. In the silence it seemed that all America had been listening to the words of the Declaration. The Speaker asked whether there was any objection to the Declaration as amended. There was none. It was put to the vote and adopted.

John Hancock, as president of the Third Continental Congress, signed it on behalf of that body. The scratching of his quill pen could be distinctly heard in the room in which the shadows were beginning to gather.

The work was done. Britain was a foreign power whose troops must be driven from the soil of the new nation which had proclaimed itself to the world as the United States of America.

"We must all hang together," said Ben Franklin solemnly, "or assuredly we shall all hang separately."

☆

3

The Declaration of Independence was first read to the people of the new country—the United States of America—on July 8, 1776.

The four days between the signing and the reading were needed to copy the document with all its amendments in a good hand, and see that it was worded exactly as it had been approved. It was read from a platform in the State House yard, which had been erected for the purpose of observing the transit of Venus—that is, the passage of the planet Venus across the face of the sun—on June 3, 1769. This is an event which occurs only four times in every 243 years and is thus of great importance to astronomers. Captain James Cook, the explorer and navigator, had gone to Tahiti to observe the transit of Venus from that island at the time.

Jefferson, present with the other members of the

Congress, listening to the Declaration being read slowly by Colonel John Nixon of a Philadelphia militia company, each word distinctly pronounced, thought of the original purpose for which the platform had been erected. Those who had seen Venus cross the face of the sun described it as a little black dot challenging the sun's power as it passed before it from rim to rim.

Jefferson turned to Franklin, who was standing by him. "We are like Venus and the sun," he said. "Opposing ourselves to the greatest power in the universe."

"Venus survived," said Franklin and Jefferson smiled. Ben Franklin, whatever the occasion, always had a quip with a grain of sense concealed in it. Jefferson had known Franklin only a little while but, like many others, began to look on him as a father. His own father had died in his youth. He loved and admired Franklin who, for all his eminence, honored by such institutions as Oxford University in England, had time to talk with men of any condition.

During the terrible days when Tom Jefferson had been torn in his mind over the decision whether or not to separate from England, it was Franklin who had comforted him over the need for the step. He told Jefferson that one of the men who had been responsible for the trial and beheading of King Charles I of England after the English Civil War, asked if he was not fearful at striking off the head of a king, had replied, "Rebellion to tyrants is obedience to God."

Jefferson was so struck by these words that he took

★

them as his motto and had a ring made with the words engraved around the edge of a large stone set in its center. He wore the ring for the rest of his life.

When the Declaration was read, the Pennsylvania militia, reckless of the need to ration gunpowder, fired volley after volley in salute to the new Republic and cheer upon cheer rose from the throng of people of all conditions who had gathered for the reading. The crowd was a representation in miniature of the nation that had just been born. There were apprentices and their masters, merchants and mechanics, farmers and frontiersmen, longshoremen and lawyers, trappers and tradesmen. Some were dressed in the best English worsted and some in deerskins, for western Pennsylvania was then the frontier. Some could read Greek and Hebrew and Latin and some could not read at all. But they were all mixed up together and they cheered together the pledge that they would defend their independence with their lives, their fortunes and their sacred honor.

The bells in every church started to ring, the pealing led by the great bell in the State House, which was to become known later as the Liberty Bell, as the State House itself was to become known as Independence Hall. All through the night the bells rang, relays of bell ringers taking over from each other.

The Royal Arms of Great Britain were taken down from the State House and burned, and similar scenes were repeated in all the states of the new Union. The printers of Philadelphia worked late hours turning out hundreds of copies of the Declaration on their presses. They were bundled up, the ink still wet, and thrust into saddlebags to be carried by riders to every corner of the new nation.

John Hancock had on July 5 sent a special copy of the Declaration to General Washington, whose headquarters were then in New York City. Washington ordered the brigades of his army to be assembled and the Declaration read to soldiers. The men of the Continental Army, as it was still called, reacted with the same joy as had the citizens of Philadelphia. There was at the time a gilded leaden statue of King George III, mounted on a horse, at Bowling Green. Washington's soldiers pulled it down and melted the lead. A few weeks later they were firing bullets made from the statue of the King at the King's soldiers in the Battle of Long Island.

When the celebration of the first Fourth of July ended in Philadelphia, the Congress turned to other work. A country had been brought into being, but it had no rules for its government, nothing to define the relationship between the thirteen separate states and the central authority; nothing to state how taxes were to be raised, on what basis they were to be levied, who was to be entitled to vote and who was not.

The United States of America existed as a title at the top of the Declaration of Independence, in a Congress of delegates, and in an army of volunteers that now faced the best disciplined troops of Europe.

★

The Congress then turned to the task of establishing the United States as a functioning government with powers defined and apportioned. Perhaps out of a sense of mercy, the task of drawing up a plan of confederation stating the relationship between the separate states and the central government, was entrusted to John Dickinson. Many members of the Congress sympathized with and admired him. He had led in the fight against the Stamp Act, drafting the "Declaration of Rights" of the Stamp Act Congress. He had drafted two "Petitions to the King" protesting against the royal policy in the American colonies and had been known as the "Penman of the Revolution." And yet he had not been able to take the final step and support the Declaration of Independence.

He was then given the task of outlining a plan for the confederation of the states into a national government, to provide him with a chance of re-establishing his reputation before the public. Dickinson went to the task eagerly. He had a quick legal mind and wrote with ease. He had the job done in a week but the Congress was not impressed with the result.

"It suffers from the vice of all his writing," said Edward Rutledge of South Carolina. "It refutes too much." In short the hesitancy natural to a highly trained lawyer, who suspects pitfalls where others see only solid ground, proved Dickinson's downfall. In the months that followed, he lost more and more of his popularity until the former "Penman of the Revolu-

★

tion" was talked of as if he were a traitor to the American cause.

But Dickinson was a better man than his critics. Unable to sacrifice his conscience for his country, he was nonetheless ready to sacrifice his life for it. He joined the Continental Army as a common soldier and fought with distinction in the bloody bitter battles that lay ahead.

Meanwhile Tom Jefferson was burning to get back to Virginia. Virginia was his home state and his great love. He had been three months in Philadelphia and during that time he knew that Virginia was framing a new state constitution. Here was the great opportunity to put into effect in his home state the principles of democracy which he cherished and for which he had fought in court and Congress.

The work of the Declaration of Independence done, he spent long hours at his writing desk in the bricklayer's house, putting down his thoughts on the constitution for Virginia.

He wanted written into that constitution guarantees of absolute freedom of religion and of the press. He wanted to put an end to the importation of slaves into Virginia. He wanted the death penalty abolished in Virginia except as punishment for the crimes of murder or serious and willful infringement of military orders. He wanted all children, including girls, to have equal rights in inheriting property. Under the old laws, only land owners could vote. Jefferson wanted the government of Virginia to give fifty acres, purchased from the Indians, to all landless men, so that they too could vote.

All these ideas he put down in the form of a constitution for Virginia. He sent copies to George Wythe, an old friend under whom he had studied law, and to Edmund Pendleton, president of the Virginia convention which was meeting to draft the state's constitution.

But Jefferson's proposals arrived too late. Tired with lengthy debate, the Virginia convention had already approved a constitution for the state and was not prepared to reopen hearings to discuss Jefferson's proposals.

When Jefferson heard of this from Wythe, his anxiety to get back to Virginia increased. He didn't like what he heard of the new constitution. The two houses of the legislature—Senate and House of Delegates—seemed to him too closely linked. They should be more independent and so balance each other. That was his opinion. He believed that if he got back to Virginia he could introduce bills in the House of Delegates which would remedy some of the faults in the new constitution.

He had personal and pressing reasons for wanting to return to his home as well. His wife Martha had been expecting a baby when he had left his home in Monticello the previous May. Now she wrote that she had lost the baby and she was ill. She wanted him back

★

home. She was lonely and weak and needed him. Surely there were others who could take over his work in Congress now and permit him to join her?

He wrote to Edmund Pendleton asking to be recalled. His request was not heeded.

In desperation, he wrote to Richard Henry Lee to come to Philadelphia and take his place in the Congress. "For God's sake, for your country's sake and for my sake, come," he wrote in his anguish. "I receive by every post such accounts of the state of Mrs. Jefferson's health that it will be impossible for me to disappoint her expectation of seeing me . . . on the eleventh of next month (August). . . . I pray you to come. I am under a sacred obligation to go home."

But still he was made to stay, working on the problem of the design of a Great Seal for the United States, on what was to be done with the Indians, on questions of taxation and commerce and money for the new Republic.

He tried to put aside his personal agony and he worked away in the little parlor of the bricklayer's house where he always went when he had any writing to do. The bricklayer's wife fretted over whether he was getting enough sleep and enough to eat. He seemed thin and when she retired for the night she could see the gleam of candlelight from under the door. In the mornings when she cleaned the parlor, the candles were gutted to stubs, the smell of them heavy in the room, and there were books in piles about the place. She thanked God that her husband was a

bricklayer. You couldn't lay bricks until two and three
o'clock in the morning.

Still Jefferson had to stay in Congress. His term as
a delegate expired August 11 but he was reappointed
for another year. The days dragged by and he almost
dreaded the arrival of the post for each time it brought
a letter from his wife asking when he would return.
His only daughter Patsy (her real name was Martha,
after her mother) was three and wanted to know when
he would be back. Finally Jefferson took matters in his
own hands. He had not only been appointed a delegate to the Congress, but he had been elected by his
county to the new House of Delegates in Virginia.

He talked with Franklin and Franklin said, "Char-
ity, it is well known, begins at home. And it might be
argued that that is where duty begins too."

Jefferson resigned his seat in the Congress, packed
his papers and his portable writing desk into his saddlebags, said goodbye to the bricklayer and his wife
and headed for Monticello. The journey was nearly
three hundred miles and it had to be made on horseback. He rode forty miles a day, until his horse could
go no more. He was in a hurry and sometimes took the
road and sometimes cut across country. He got back to
Monticello on September 8 and Martha, his wife, was
waiting for him, pale but happy.

"They let you come?" she asked.

Jefferson shook his head. "I came without them let-
ting me," he said and took her in his arms.

Patsy was a little nervous in the presence of the tall

★
35

thin man who was embracing her mother, who seemed to be crying. She wasn't quite sure that she wanted him to pick her up just yet. She wanted to defer the moment until she was a little more used to him.

"Papa," she said in an attempt to stall his picking her up, "there's a dawn in the trees."

"A dawn?" asked Jefferson, turning to her.

"She means a fawn," said his wife.

"No, my dear," said Jefferson. "She means a dawn. There is a dawn in the trees." He turned to look at the woodlands which he loved, the forest tumbling up the mountains to the west.

There seemed to be a special light upon them. He was home and there was, indeed, a dawn in the trees.

4

Jefferson had almost three weeks of happiness at his home in Monticello. His wife's health improved daily. His very presence seemed to give her strength. The great mansion which he had started building nine years before and on which he would work for many years to come, had been gloomy while he was away. Now there were smiles on the faces of the house slaves and joking in the kitchen. Tawney, the old mulatto who had been specially bequeathed to Tom Jefferson by his father in his will, said even the copper pots in the scullery were smiling because the master was back.

"Sun ain't warm no more when master's away," said Tawney, and that was the way they all felt, for Tom Jefferson never beat or harshly punished a slave in his life and they all loved him.

He loved riding and, the day after his three-hundred-mile trip from Philadelphia, decided to ride one of his thoroughbred hunters. The horse was led from the stables and Tom Jefferson stood back and eyed it closely. Saddle, stirrup leathers, stirrups, bridle and bit were polished to a high shine and the gelding's golden coat was gleaming. The hoofs were clean and the mane and tail beautifully combed. He took a handkerchief from his sleeve, passed it over the horse's coat and looked at it.

"Clean as a dinner plate, Master Tom," said the groom, grinning. Jefferson smiled. Not a speck of dirt showed on the handkerchief.

"Fit to ride," he said, for he would not mount a horse of his own that was not in immaculate condition. He put his foot in the stirrup and Patsy, who had got over her shyness, said, "Papa, can I come?" From his seat in the saddle on the back of the big hunter, she looked like a tiny anxious doll.

"Of course," said Jefferson and nodded to the groom who handed his little daughter up to him. He seated her on the saddle before him and they set out. Every day after that he took Patsy riding with him.

It was the greatest fun for her—frightening and yet exciting and wonderful. Seated on the saddle before her tall father, she seemed very high up. The ground, when they went into a canter, sped by her so fast she couldn't really see the stones or the grass or the low brush. All was a blur. And the wind caressed her face and her hair came undone and streamed back as if someone was pulling it gently.

★

The first few rides Tom Jefferson took with his daughter he walked the horse. But after a little while she wanted to go faster and soon they would gallop. Then Patsy wanted the horse to gallop all the time and Jefferson had to point out to her that the horse had to rest sometime.

The two were inseparable—the man six foot two and lean and the tiny doll of a girl who had to reach up to hold his hand. As his wife grew stronger, Jefferson encouraged her to come for short walks and then rides with him. They went together around the grounds, talking about a fountain that was to be put in the center of the lawn, and a marble bench in an arbor that they planned together and would be a special place for them. The weather was glorious and the trees—maple, beech and oak—beginning to turn so that the forest glowed in reds and yellows and dark greens.

There was always company for dinner and Jefferson's favorite guest was Philip Mazzei, an Italian from Tuscany who had come to America some years previously. Mazzei was originally the friend of Thomas Adams of Williamsburg and it was Adams who introduced him to Jefferson.

He was a man of standing in his own country, for he was a doctor who had practiced medicine in Turkey and had been ambassador of the Grand Duke of Tuscany in London where he had been friendly with Ben Franklin.

When Adams brought Mazzei to meet Jefferson, the

★

two took to each other immediately. Jefferson insisted that Mazzei stay the night at Monticello. He was surprised to find that Mazzei spoke English fluently and Mazzei was surprised to find that Jefferson spoke Italian fluently. The two were up early the next morning before anyone else in the household was awake. They went for a walk together and Mazzei said he wanted to try to grow wine grapes in Virginia and raise wheat for export.

Jefferson was immediately intrigued. When they returned from their walk, he had given Mazzei two thousand acres of land on which to raise grapes and wheat and the Italian, who had come for the night, stayed instead for years, building a house close to Monticello and cultivating his land.

The man fascinated Jefferson, though Jefferson could not get along with Mazzei's wife. She was ignorant, grasping and gossipy and Jefferson had a hard time being polite to her.

But Jefferson liked Mazzei, and he had sent him a copy of his Declaration of Independence as soon as it was approved by the Congress. Now, at the dinner table, they talked of crops and weather and grapes and wine and music, the rights of man and the needs of the soil, and Martha Jefferson listened with an awe that never left her to this astonishing husband who at thirty-three years of age could talk with knowledge on any subject on earth and with any man.

"Madam," said Mazzei, "you are married to a genius.

★

I do not pay him a compliment. I state a fact. Tell me, how long has he been playing the violin?"

"For many years—he practices three hours a day."

"And how long has he been interested in agriculture?"

"For many years—long before I met him."

"And in architecture?"

"Since he was a boy."

"And law and philosophy and economics and currency and medicine and the language of the Indians?"

Martha Jefferson laughed. "He has always been interested in all these things," she said.

"And no doubt he practices them three hours a day? But there are not that many hours in a day. That is why I say he is a genius without fear of being wrong. A genius can achieve in one hour of work what would be the labor of a week for another. When I first came here to meet Mr. Jefferson, I expected to find a man of perhaps a little extra learning. Nothing more. But I have found Socrates in the wilderness."

"Come, sir," said Martha Jefferson. "This is hardly the wilderness."

"It was the wilderness, madam," said Mazzei, "until Thomas Jefferson tamed it."

There was truth in that, for Jefferson at Monticello had built, on what was but a short time before the frontier of Virginia, a mansion as stately as any to be found in Europe. But it was far more modern than any other such mansion.

★

Doors were balanced so as to open at the slightest touch. The clock in the entrance hall told not only the time but also the day of the week. The mechanics for telling the day of the week was operated by cannonballs and it tickled Tom Jefferson, who hated bloodshed, to be thus turning the sword into a plowshare in his own way.

Between pantry and dining room was a revolving door with shelves to quicken the service of dinner and keep the heat and smells of the kitchen from the dining quarters. The revolving door also saved work for the servants. A dumbwaiter between the ground floor and his study made it easy to send up his meals without disturbing him while he was writing—for he could not abide being interrupted at work.

He liked to know from which direction the wind was blowing, but didn't always have time to go outside to look at the weathercock on the roof. So he put a pointer on the bottom of the weathercock so that the direction and strength of the wind was recorded on a dial on the ceiling of his parlor. He put a parquet floor (this is a floor of inlaid wood, in patterns) in his drawing room and it was the marvel of America, being the first of its kind ever seen in the country.

The older plantation houses of Virginia, some of them charming but built without benefit of architect, were spoiled by a clutter of other buildings and rooms that surrounded them—the laundry room, kitchen, storerooms, icehouse and so on. All these were necessary adjuncts of the main building, but often took on the appearance of a number of squalid shacks.

Jefferson solved the problem of providing these necessary structures without spoiling the handsome appearance of Monticello by putting them underground. He even put the servants' quarters underground and designed an efficient ventilating system for them. There they were sheltered from blizzard and blazing sun, his heating bill in wintertime was greatly reduced, and his house servants did not have to walk through rain or snow to get to their quarters and so their health was better.

Over the tops of all these buildings he put terraces and walks so that Monticello was not surrounded by a ragged hodgepodge of structures, but by beautifully landscaped gardens, and had a grace and elegance unrivaled to this day.

Nobody of course taught Tom Jefferson architecture. He studied the art himself, sending to Europe for books on building styles. He learned carpentry, plumbing, bricklaying, the problems of stress on arches and on pillars. When he needed a new key for a lock he cut it out of metal himself with a file, and when a particular kind of lock was not obtainable he made it.

Around Monticello he planted orchards of peaches and apples and cherries and Mazzei worked with him in trying to get oranges to grow in Virginia. They raised some but they were sour. Jefferson made what is now called marmalade out of them. He grew all his

★

43

own vegetables and had a pond stocked with trout, for he liked to produce his own food.

Life, liberty and the pursuit of happiness—these were the rights Tom Jefferson had asserted belonged to all men. He found them in Monticello, raising his own food, building his own house, reading his books, riding, playing his violin and talking until late at night with any guest who visited him.

He had almost three weeks of this kind of life and then—Martha being now much stronger—he took her and Patsy off to Williamsburg to consult Dr. Brydon over his wife's health. They stayed in George Wythe's house in Williamsburg. Dr. Brydon said there was nothing constitutionally wrong with Mrs. Jefferson. She needed rest and he advised Jefferson to stay as much with his wife as he could.

"A wife, sir," said Dr. Brydon, "is but half a creature when her husband is away."

"A husband, sir," replied Jefferson, "is but half a creature when away from his wife."

Tom Jefferson resolved to keep Martha by his side so he could take care of her. But the decision was hardly made before pressure was put on him to break it—pressure coming from the Congress of the United States.

One of the principal objects of the Declaration of Independence had been to serve notice to the world that the United States was now an independent nation with no ties whatever with Great Britain, and thus in a position to enter into alliances with other powers.

The other power that Congress had specifically in

★

44

mind was France. Everybody knew that an alliance with France was desperately needed if the Revolutionary War was to be won. Hardly had the Declaration been approved and Jefferson left Philadelphia for Monticello when the Congress voted to appoint commissioners to the court of the French King.

Their job would be to persuade France to help in the war against England—help in the first instance by supplying the materials of war and finally by openly joining in the struggle. The commissioners were selected by ballot and when the results of the balloting were announced, the men picked as commissioners to France were Ben Franklin, Silas Deane and Tom Jefferson.

A courier was sent to Jefferson to inform him of his appointment. The courier carried a sealed letter in which Jefferson was informed that the mission to France was to be kept a close secret. The vessel on which the commissioners were to sail was not to be announced and Jefferson was to inform the president of the Congress, John Hancock, what port he would leave from and at what time a ship should be sent to take him to France.

The United States in 1776 had but a tiny navy, consisting only of merchant ships converted for war and a few sloops of war captured in daring raids from the British. So important was the commission to France that one of these vessels was assigned to take the commissioners there. But date and place of sailing had to be kept secret lest the powerful British navy, whose

★

45

warships and frigates swarmed around the coast, sink the vessel.

Hard on the heels of the message from Congress came a letter from Richard Henry Lee to Jefferson. "The plan of foreign treaty is just finished, and yourself and Dr. Franklin and Mr. Deane, now in France, as the trustees to execute this all important business. . . . In my judgment, the most eminent services that the greatest of her sons can do America will not more essentially serve her and honor themselves than a successful negotiation with France. With this country everything depends upon it."

And there it was. The need for a French alliance was desperate. The need for Tom Jefferson to stay with his wife was equally desperate, and she was too weak still to take the long sea voyage to France with him.

For three days Jefferson could not make up his mind what reply to send to the Congress. For three days he kept the congressional messenger waiting while he debated the matter, torn between the love of his wife and the needs of his country.

From early youth, trained by gentle George Wythe, he had learned to submit all problems to reason and put emotions aside as unreliable counselors. But here was a problem in which his emotions were so deeply involved that they could not be put aside. And yet, by the process of reason, he finally arrived at his decision.

The mission to France would not fail because of his absence. There were others who could go, men older than he and men versed in diplomacy and capable of

★
46

speaking French as fluently as he. On the other hand, no one could take his place with Martha. So he wrote Hancock a letter, painfully worded, begging to be excused from the mission to France.

"No cares for my own person, nor yet for my private affairs, would have induced one moment's hesitation to accept the charge," he wrote. "But circumstances very peculiar in the situation of my family, such as neither permit me to leave nor carry it [his family with him to France] compel me to ask leave to decline a service so honorable and at the same time so important to the American cause. The necessity under which I labor and the conflict I have undergone for three days, during which I could not determine to dismiss your messenger, will, I hope, plead my pardon with Congress."

Hancock understood and Ben Franklin went to France to attempt to persuade a Catholic monarchy to come to the aid of a Protestant republic. It was the kind of job that wise old Ben Franklin was eminently fitted to undertake.

The day after writing to John Hancock, Jefferson took his seat in the House of Delegates of the Virginia legislature.

While he had been riding with Patsy at Monticello and talking with Philip Mazzei about rice farming in Italy, and with a new bricklayer, Randolph Johnson, on mixing mortar, his mind had been busy also with the defects in the new constitution of Virginia. The constitution was now the law. But he made notes on a

★

number of bills he wanted to introduce in the House of Delegates to make the state more democratic.

Many of the laws on the statute books of Virginia had been taken over, unaltered by as much as a comma, from the old colonial laws administered by the British. Jefferson knew Virginia law thoroughly and knew too that some of these laws were vicious and should be repealed or amended. He couldn't change the constitution, but he could try to change some of the laws on the statute books.

When he took his seat in the House of Delegates on October 11, 1776, he wasn't Tom Jefferson, agriculturalist, philosopher, musician and architect. He was Tom Jefferson, reformer, defender of the rights of people who could never own a home like Monticello, who could never hope for the influence that was his to command as a prominent figure in Virginia aristocracy.

To achieve this, Tom Jefferson had to declare war on his own class, take violent issue with his wealthy friends at whose lavish dining room tables he had sat, drinking French wines from Venetian glasses resting on tablecloths of Chantilly lace. He had to wrest from his friends privileges and influence which their families had enjoyed for over a hundred years. Some never forgave him and looked upon him as a traitor to his own kind—a man set upon the ruination of all that was good in Virginia. But Jefferson was undaunted.

At the opening of the legislature, it was expected that no important business would be enacted. But Jefferson had hardly exchanged greetings with his friends,

★

taken his seat, and gained the eye of the Speaker when he asked leave to introduce a bill for the establishment and organization of new courts of justice in Virginia. His motion was approved. Virginia was well aware that the old courts needed revision. Jefferson was certainly the man to work on that problem.

The big surprise came the next day. Jefferson was again on his feet asking leave to bring in another bill, this time one of a revolutionary character. The greater portions of the rich land in Virginia, obtained in the early days for little or nothing, were held in what was called fee tail. Fee tail meant that the owner could not divide his land among his sons and daughters. All had to go to one descendant.

Another land law, primogeniture, provided that when a man died without making a will, all his property went to his eldest son.

The effect of the two laws was to produce in Virginia a landed aristocracy who possessed enormous wealth through inheritance. Because of their wealth, these families had great influence and it was from them that the judges, legislators and other rulers of the state had been drawn in the past. These families constituted an aristocracy of wealth. Jefferson wanted to replace this with an aristocracy of the mind.

His bill would make it illegal for land in the future to be deeded in this manner. Big estates must be divided among all the children of a family, as the current owner decided, and this division would eventually dissolve the great wealthy families of Virginia. There

★

would be no big single land owners, but instead a vast number of people owning sufficient land to support themselves. Government would be handed over to the people instead of being passed from generation to generation to a privileged few.

No single piece of legislation that Tom Jefferson introduced during the whole of his life aroused such animosity against him as this bill. The great families of Virginia—the Randolphs, the Carters, the Pages—to most of whom Tom Jefferson was related either by blood or marriage, saw in this one measure the utter destruction of their privileged position.

Edmund Pendleton, whose influence was great as Speaker of the House of Delegates, led the opposition to the bill and it was vigorous. Pendleton, a warm friend of Jefferson's, was an able debater and a formidable opponent. He had not the fiery style nor the flights of moving fancy of Patrick Henry. His tactics were always painstaking and studied. If he lost the main issue, he concentrated on one detail and gained that. Then he attacked another detail. By the process of winning on details it was often found, when all was done, that Pendleton had in effect won on the main issue.

Day after day Jefferson, called a traitor to his own kind, battled Pendleton and other influential delegates, fighting to abolish these laws. For eleven days he argued his case while Pendleton would concede in one area and then attack in another.

"He's like a will o' the wisp," Tom Jefferson told

★

Martha. "I can never tell when I have won, when I am rid of him. He retreats from one position only to reappear in another. Indeed, when he grants me a point I am unsure whether I have achieved a victory or suffered some hidden loss."

Patrick Henry, now governor of Virginia, was not there to help Jefferson in these debates. Nor was George Wythe who was still in Philadelphia as a delegate to the Congress. Jefferson had to fight what was largely a lone battle.

When finally it seemed that he had won on the issue of land held in fee tail—that is, land which could be deeded only to one person—Pendleton introduced what seemed to be a minor and reasonable amendment.

"I have been beaten on every point by my amiable friend Mr. Jefferson," he said, smiling at Tom, for the two held each other in the highest respect and never doubted each other's motives. "Mr. Jefferson is a reasonable man and has always been the first to defend, and properly defend, the rights of others against harsh or seemingly unjust laws. He will then have no objection, I am sure, to defending the right of a land owner to deed all his land to one descendant with a provision that it is not to be divided in any way by that descendant, if he so wishes."

"I am sorry," said Jefferson, immediately spotting the trap. "But I do object. This provision seemingly so innocent, and so just, would in effect destroy the whole reform which I am so earnestly seeking. My

★

whole desire is to take land out of the control of those who are long dead and put it under the control of those who are living, giving them the right to dispose of it as they will.

"Can any gentleman explain to this House why a man dead twenty, forty or a hundred years should still have control over the disposal of huge acreages of land in Virginia today? Can any gentleman give me a good reason why when a man inherits a piece of land, he must be bound in disposing of it by a grandfather or a great-grandfather long gone from this earth? Are we to be ruled, gentlemen, by the dead or by the living? That is the nub of the question."

Jefferson's words were well received by the younger delegates, many of them denied by the old laws any share of their ancestral estates. Pendleton's amendment was defeated by only a few ballots, but the holding of land in fee tail was abolished in Virginia in a bloodless land reform instituted by Jefferson.

Next came the law of primogeniture—the law that said that if a man died without a will, his land must go to his eldest son, the rest getting nothing. Again Pendleton fought aganist any change and again Tom Jefferson had to argue the case sentence by sentence, word by word, comma by comma.

At one point Pendleton proposed that in the case of a man dying without a will, the eldest son should receive at least twice as much as any of the others.

"You will surely have no objection to such a provision," he said to Jefferson. "The eldest son is the head of the family. His position as head of the family is confirmed in scripture and in civilized custom. He should get at least twice what the others get."

"I will have no objection, sir," said Tom, "if you can prove to me that the eldest son eats twice as much as the second eldest, that he needs twice as many clothes, twice as much money and twice as big a house." Pendleton lost that point and eventually the law of primogeniture went with the law of fee tail.

Such a sweeping victory over established and crippling custom would have been more than enough for ordinary men. But it was only a start for reformer Tom Jefferson.

He turned to slavery, which he abominated. He introduced a bill aimed at the gradual abolishment of slavery. The bill provided that the children of slaves were to be born free, and were to be educated at the state expense. When they grew up, they were to be settled in communities where they would be utterly free of the taint of slavery. The proposal got nowhere.

"How can they talk of freedom and buy and sell their fellow human beings?" Jefferson cried in anguish to his wife when his bill was defeated. "If they believe God is just, are they not afraid to face Him as masters of slaves?"

On the issue of slavery he would not be comforted. He fought it all his life and achieved one real victory. He was able to get the Virginia legislature to pass a law prohibiting the importation of new slaves into the colony. That ended the degrading spectacle of the slave market where male slaves were sold as "bucks" and their wives as "fillies." But an inner anguish over the existence of slavery remained with Tom Jefferson to the day of his death.

He had reformed the land laws. He had done what he could about slavery. But he was not finished. He turned to the church. The Church of England was the official church of Virginia. Its clerics were supported by taxation of the people, even though those paying taxes were Quakers or Presbyterians or Catholics.

Many of these clerics became rich land owners who attended church only on Sunday and did little to guide the spiritual life even of their official congregations. Furthermore, there was no religious toleration under the law as it stood in Virginia. It was a crime to hold a religious conviction which differed from that of the Church of England. It was a crime not to go to church and it was a crime to attend any service other than that of the Church of England. Jefferson fought against all these injustices until finally he had obtained for Virginia what was finally to be obtained for the nation—separation of Church and State and freedom of worship.

Still it was not enough.

He pressed for and obtained the rewriting of all the laws of the colony so that they were put into a language anyone of a reasonable education could understand. Here Pendleton was his ally and George Wythe, returning from Philadelphia, worked with them on a committee which in a short time reduced shelves of

★

law books to 126 clearly written laws that filled only ninety printed pages.

In this rewriting of the language of the laws, Jefferson was able, with his colleagues, to obtain a revision of their contents. The death penalty for all crimes but murder and treason was abolished. He introduced a bill to provide free schools for children. They were to get three years' free instruction in reading, writing and arithmetic, and the best of the children were to go on to higher schools. Finally, the cream of the crop were to get a free education at William and Mary College.

This education bill Jefferson regarded as all-important. It would develop and train the talents and minds of the young people of Virginia and help them to vote and govern themselves wisely. This was what Jefferson aimed at when he talked of replacing an aristocracy of wealth with an aristocracy of the mind. But his education bill was partially approved. He succeeded in getting a form of free primary schooling for the children of Virginia.

And so Jefferson, the reformer, went on with his work, building the Republic of America from the ground up—from Virginia the state to America the nation.

But in the midst of all this work he could not forget Monticello. His home always called him. He went back as often as he could. And on April 1, 1777, an event took place at Monticello that filled him with happiness.

He had planted some cherry and peach trees and,

★

rounding a bend in the garden, found their branches powdered with blossoms. He hurried back to tell Martha. "They are in bloom," he said. "The buds opened with the sun." There were tears of pleasure in his eyes at the coming of spring.

5

Meanwhile the bitter flood of war was rolling over New England. Boston was liberated in March only for New York to fall in September.

Overwhelmingly outnumbered, the Continental Army was driven off Long Island and then Manhattan Island, and straggled south to put the Delaware River between itself and its foes. Washington's credit with his countrymen fell to almost nothing. Even staunch men began to doubt his ability and wondered whether he ought not to be replaced by someone of more military experience like Charles Lee. Among the doubters were men of integrity like Dr. Benjamin Rush, signer of the Declaration of Independence, a friend of Jefferson and one of the most advanced medical men of his day.

The war news reached Virginia only after long delays. Washington kept in close correspondence with Patrick Henry, governor of the state, and Henry and the Virginians supported Washington to the fullest in every request he made for men and arms.

Patrick Henry now lived in the large governor's mansion in Williamsburg. He took no great pleasure in the place. He still spoke with an up-country accent and dreamed of the times he had gone roving through the Virginia forests with a powder horn slung around his shoulders and a gun cradled in his arms, hunting game. He disliked ceremony and hated writing. He was in his early forties and had to wear glasses now. He attributed the impairment of his eyesight to the amount of reading he had had to do as a lawyer and member of both the Virginia legislature and the Continental Congress.

Jefferson smiled over this for the fact was that he, Jefferson, did ten times as much reading as Patrick Henry. Of course, he was seven years younger. But if reading was a factor in failing eyesight, then Jefferson would certainly have to wear glasses, and he didn't.

Once Patrick Henry, a guest at Monticello, had looked over Jefferson's huge and growing library and, somewhat abashed, announced that he ought to read more. He was of a fiery temperament and when he made a decision he wanted to do something about it then and there. So he borrowed from Jefferson two volumes of the essays of Hume and swore that, by thunder, before he returned them, he would have read every mortal word they contained. But he brought them back on his next visit and confessed that he'd hardly been able to get through two or three chapters.

"He's as dull a dog as ever picked up a pen," he complained. Then he added lamely, "Well, he seems dull to me."

Patrick Henry's mind was active, questing, adventurous and fretted under closely reasoned arguments. He developed, while governor, a little cabinet of advisers and the men he chose were both his friends and great readers to boot—making up for his own deficiency in that area of learning.

Jefferson was one of this group and so were George Wythe and George Mason; the latter had drafted the Virginia Constitution and was a lifelong friend of George Washington. (There was a predominance of men named George in America in those days, a testimony of the former loyalty to the English kings. After the Revolution the name fell into disfavor.)

Virginia, like all seaboard states, had its own war problem. There were over a thousand miles of navigable sea coast in the state, all utterly without protection. An effort was made to create a state naval force to protect the towns and seamen but the problem was, all in all, beyond the resources of Virginia.

Exposed on the eastern coast to royalist raids, Virginia's western frontier was open to the attacks of the English and Indians. Pioneering families had pushed westward into what is now Kentucky, but was then part of Virginia. Little settlements were started here and there. The Indians, encouraged by the British,

★

menaced the settlers, who had no one to protect them. They did not indeed know where to turn for help. Were they part of the state of Virginia? Should they establish a government of their own? How were they to get arms and powder to protect themselves? These were the questions these settlers faced—orphans of the frontier, abandoned, they felt, to the savagery of Indian warfare.

Then one day a young man in deerskins and carrying a long rifle came into Williamsburg. He had come, he said, to take his seat in the Virginia legislature because he had been elected to it. He gave his name as George Rogers Clark and, when pressed, gave his age as twenty-four.

The Virginia legislature was not then in session and Clark was advised to see Governor Patrick Henry about his election. He asked for an interview and got one readily; soon the two were seated together in the great mansion that suited neither of them. They talked of the frontier from which George Rogers Clark had come.

"There's a place called Harrod's Town," said Clark. "It's on the other side of the Cumberlands in the area the Indians call Kentucky. A lot of Virginians have been roving over the mountains and they built this place. Well, there was a meeting held there, June 6, and me and John Gabriel Jones were elected delegates to the Virginia Assembly and that's why I'm here."

Patrick Henry was delighted. The whole thing of course was as illegal as it was bold and that appealed to him. The area vaguely known as Kentucky had no right to elect a delegate to the Virginia legislature.

"You know," said Henry, "that this whole thing—your being elected as a delegate to our Legislature—is as weak a case as ever I have been asked to embrace."

"I do," said George Rogers Clark.

"And what do you have to say further about it?"

"Nothing—except that the more desperate it seems, the more it pleases me," was the reply.

"By thunder," said Henry, "and me too." But he could not take it upon himself to admit Kentucky into the state of Virginia as a political entity. He called his official council together to debate the problem.

The council ordered that Clark be supplied with five hundred pounds of gunpowder for the defense of the people of Kentucky and a little later, with the approval of the legislature, Kentucky became a county of Virginia, its inhabitants protected by Virginia's laws and wealth. George Rogers Clark returned to Kentucky with the news of its admission formally to the state of Virginia and a year later he was back in Williamsburg with a plan that shook even Patrick Henry.

In brief, he wanted to open up the war on the frontier, attacking the British garrisons on the Ohio and forever destroying the British and Indian menace to the western frontier of Virginia. He would need men, materials and money for the job and he came to ask for them at a time when Virginia was desperately short of all three herself.

★

Clark arrived back in Williamsburg on November 5, 1777. This time he didn't go directly to see Governor Patrick Henry. He kept his frontiersman's ears open for remarks and talk that would tell him how Patrick Henry and the council would react to his plan. It was really a plan whereby Virginia, already supplying men and arms to the Continental Army, would go to war in the West and go to war alone. None of the other states was likely to join in. Virginia, represented by twenty-five-year-old George Rogers Clark, would attack England in the West so that when the Revolutionary War was won, the road would be open for American expansion westward—not blockaded by Britain.

For a while Clark hung around the clubs and streets and taverns of Williamsburg, listening to the talk and sounding the people out on their reaction to opening the war on the western frontier.

He had a frontiersman's sense of strategy, even in political matters. He had taken part in a lot of councils with both whites and red men and knew what an advantage it was to have powerful allies when he wanted to win a particular point. He called on Tom Jefferson who was from western Virginia, like himself, and whose family were pioneers as Clark's family were pioneers. Indeed the Clark family home was not far from Monticello.

Jefferson was nine years older than George Rogers Clark, who had hardly finished exchanging formalities with him before he had unrolled a map of the Ohio

Valley containing portions of the Mississippi. He pointed to the British forts along the rivers.

"As you see, sir," he said, "the British cut us off from the West which is a natural direction in which we have to expand—to the Mississippi, and maybe beyond. More than that, the British governor at Detroit, Henry Hamilton, has roused all the Indian tribes—Sioux, Chippewas, Sauk and Fox, Winnebagos, Potawatomis and Menominees—and they are on the warpath. Over the Cumberland gap, there isn't one of our settlements that is safe. We have to fight back or be wiped out and when the war ends Britain will claim the West even if she loses her thirteen colonies in the East."

Jefferson knew something of the country of which young red-haired George Rogers Clark was speaking. In his extensive law practice, when he was younger, he had represented many of the settlers in establishing their claims. Where others looked east to the Atlantic and to Europe for America's future, Jefferson always looked west and saw beyond the rolling horizon of the Blue Ridge and Appalachian Mountains a vast empty continent which might bring forth and nurture the greatest democracy on earth.

"What will you need, Mr. Clark?" he asked quietly.

"Very little," was the reply. "Powder, about two hundred hand-picked men, money to buy supplies and build barges for travel on the rivers—and secrecy. Secrecy is as important as powder."

★
63

Jefferson nodded. "Hand-picked men," he said. "You will need frontiersmen like yourself."

"Yes," said Clark. "Tough men who don't like roads, know the Indians and can use a hunting knife in the dark. I have my eye on most of the fellows I need. And they have particular reasons for being prepared to fight."

"Such as?" asked Jefferson.

"Well, there's Ted Lyon. His brother Daniel was killed by Indians while headed for Logan's Fort on the Green River. Then Glen Peters. He found his sister a mile out of Cumberland, dead and scalped, with her husband dead beside her. Hamilton is buying scalps from the Indians. We call him 'the Hair Buyer.' There's others—Sam Moore, Barnery Stagner—his father was killed half a mile from the fort—and so on. I won't have trouble getting my two hundred men. Most of my trouble is likely to be right here, Mr. Jefferson, getting my plan approved."

"I think not," said Jefferson. "But there are others you should talk to to gain a solid support before Governor Henry. Not that I want to suggest for one moment that Mr. Henry will not support your plan. But it will greatly strengthen his hand if you have first the support of others."

Jefferson then arranged for Clark to speak with George Mason, George Wythe and Richard Henry Lee and, when he had the support of all these men, they went with him to Governor Patrick Henry who quickly agreed to the whole proposal.

★

Clark was given a war chest of £1200 sterling and authority to raise his company of riflemen and have barges built where needed. Patrick Henry had not, as governor, the authority to give Clark £1200 for his expedition. He had to ask the Virginia legislature to vote the amount.

There was danger here of publicizing the whole plan if any of the legislators started questioning what a young frontiersman wanted with so much of the public money. But between Jefferson, Mason and George Wythe, skillful legislators all of them, the grant was slipped through as being needed for the defense of western Virginia.

His plan approved and his money voted, Clark slipped out of Williamsburg without fuss on January 4, 1778. His mission in effect was to open the West for American settlement by driving the British out. The odds against him were enormous. But that was what he liked.

Clark mustered his men and built his boats at the falls of the Ohio near present-day Louisville. He headed down river to capture what he regarded as a key British settlement, Kaskaskia, at the junction of the Kaskaskia River and the Mississippi, in what is now the state of Illinois. He shot the rapids of the Ohio and on June 28, 1778, while his party was making its way down the river in boats, the sun was slowly blotted out by an eclipse.

A boding darkness descended on the river and the forests around. Most of Clark's men were uneducated

★

and highly superstitious. They regarded the eclipse of the sun as a warning and wanted to turn back. They could face Sioux or Redcoats without a tremor but not the supernatural. They stopped paddling, staring at the slowly disappearing sun and feeling the cold shadow of the eclipse strike through their deerskins.

Some made elaborate signs of the cross, for they had a smattering of religion. Others fumbled in medicine bags obtained from the Indians; many had married Indian women. They took out pinches of ground root and animal hair and threw them on the surface of the river.

"We're doomed," cried one of the men in Clark's boat. "Not a man of us will come back up this river alive!"

"If a shadow can kill you, you are doomed all right," said Clark. "For myself, I've no fear of shadows."

"It's a sign," said the man. "A warning."

"If it's a sign," replied Clark, "then the sign is for the British and not for us. Watch your paddle there. There's rocks ahead. And get your powderhorn up higher. There's more men die of damp powder than shadows before the sun."

So he cajoled them out of the mood of despair and they went on down the river, considerably relieved when the sun reappeared. They drove the boats on down the Ohio until they came to the mouth of the Tennessee. Here they hid the boats and, landing, struck north through the forest toward Kaskaskia.

They could take no more food than each man could

★

carry and, because of the need of surprise, dared not shoot game. The last two days of the march there was not a morsel of food for any of the men.

But Kaskaskia was unguarded and fell to them without a shot being fired. The date was a significant one, July 4, 1778, the second anniversary of the Declaration of Independence. Two other settlements, Cahokia and Prairie de Rocher, surrendered to Clark without resistance, and George Rogers Clark found himself in possession of the whole territory, but without sufficient men to hold the area if there were any resistance.

The town of Vincennes, through the aid of a French priest at Kaskaskia, also surrendered to Rogers and this was a very important conquest for adjacent to Vincennes was Fort Sackville, an important frontier strong point which was now in American hands.

But now Lieutenant Colonel Henry Hamilton, the British commander in Detroit, decided to strike back. He was as bold and as tough a man as Clark. Furthermore, he was cruel and unscrupulous in waging war, for he set a bounty on scalps and encouraged the Indians to bring him the scalps of any Americans they could get. He paid the same price for a child's scalp as he paid for a man's and even joined the Indians in their war dances when they flung their tomahawks at a pole strung with human scalps.

Hamilton collected sixty Indians and about 170 soldiers and struck southward from Detroit in midwinter, determined to recapture Vincennes. The journey he undertook was appalling but he succeeded. He

★

reached Vincennes on December 17 and took the town without a struggle, for there were only one or two of Clark's men there to defend it. When news of the fall of Vincennes reached Clark at Kaskaskia, the people there were thrown into a panic.

Hamilton the Hair Buyer was so feared that some were in favor of fleeing into the wilderness and others pleaded with Clark to leave with his riflemen so that Hamilton, when he arrived, would not butcher the inhabitants of the little settlement.

Many of Clark's own men drifted off, their enlistments expired, and he had at this crisis in his campaign scarcely one hundred riflemen in his own force. But Father Gibault, the French Catholic priest who had persuaded the inhabitants of Vincennes to surrender to Clark originally, went about in Kaskaskia quietening the fears of the people. Clark thought the situation over calmly and decided to do exactly what Hamilton had done: make an impossible midwinter march and attack Vincennes with a handful of men.

He wrote a note to Patrick Henry outlining his plan; Henry showed it to Tom Jefferson. "I know the case is desperate," Clark wrote, "but, sir, we must either quit the country or attack Mr. Hamilton. . . . Who knows what fortune will do for us? Great things have been effected by a few men well conducted."

On February 7, his little army reinforced by a few volunteers, some of whom were Frenchmen who had no love of the British, Clark set out. The weather was mild and a thaw had set in so that the ground was under water in most places. But there was plenty of game and for the first few days the men were in high spirits.

At the end of a week, Clark had reached a point within twenty miles of Vincennes and now faced the crossing of the Little Wabash. Here he ran into his first real difficulty, for the early thaw had widened and deepened the river. It took two days to get across the Little Wabash. Then came the swollen Embarrass River which now had the proportions of a lake. It had flooded over its banks and hours were spent in finding a place where it could be forded. And when the Embarrass River was crossed, the Wabash itself had to be negotiated. The land between the two rivers was flooded so that it became a small stream.

Those who were too sick or exhausted to wade were put in canoes and pulled over the flooded territory by their fellows. There was no dry ground to sleep on or light a fire on. Men lay in freezing water to get a rest, fearful a rise of the flood would cause them to drown. Still they went on, their progress reduced to three miles a day—three miles not of walking or of marching but of wading waist- and shoulder-deep in flood water, with their rifles held over their heads to keep the locks dry.

On February 22 the men were all noticeably weaker and on February 23 a crisis of exhaustion arose. The men said they could not go on. Their voices were reduced to hoarse whispers. They had slept that night, shivering, in canoes and boats in the middle of the

★

flood. The prospect of getting back into the icy water and wading on to launch an impossible attack on a strongly defended fort was more than they could face. The men refused to get out of the canoes and go further.

Clark raised himself up, looked about him and slipped shoulder-deep into the flood. "Come on," he said. "Grumbling won't make you any drier." He didn't even look over his shoulder to see the effect of his words, but waded on away from the canoes. The men cursed him and said that, by thunder, they wouldn't follow him. And even while they were saying this, they got into the water and waded after him.

That day's wading was the worst of the adventure. The water was deeper and the men tripped and fell on submerged logs. Some went under, their wet deerskins making it impossible for them to swim. They were hauled to the surface by their fellows. When they found a stump of a tree sticking out of the freezing flood, the men clung to it in clusters, getting a little rest before going on. But they went on because always ahead of them was George Rogers Clark. At last the water shoaled and they reached high ground. They were but two miles from Fort Sackville and the town of Vincennes, shivering and soaking wet.

They lit fires, dried their clothes, cooked the last of their rations, measured their store of powder and decided they hadn't got enough for anything approaching a battle.

Clark was not dismayed. He captured a lone

★

Frenchman and sent him into Vincennes with a message. The message left no one in any doubt as to what he was going to do. He was going to take Vincennes and Fort Sackville. Those inhabitants of the town who sided with him should get into their houses and stay there. Those who wished to oppose him should go over and join Colonel Hamilton in Fort Sackville.

Then he rounded up his men and, with drums beating and flags flying, marched into Vincennes. The fort was set apart from the town which lay open to him. To give the impression that he had a far greater force than he actually commanded, Clark made his men march down the main street of Vincennes. They then split into columns, going down the side streets, to rejoin at the main street near the entrance of the town and go down it again.

To those at the other end of the main thoroughfare, it looked as though an endless force of Americans was pouring into the town. Some fled to Fort Sackville and announced that they had witnessed a miracle. George Rogers Clark had crossed twenty miles of flooded country in midwinter with several regiments and every man wore clothing as dry as a bone!

The news spread dismay in Fort Sackville. Clark had warned the defenders of the fort that he would attack it that night and take it within the next few hours. At sunset he marched out of Vincennes toward the fort and opened fire on its eleven-foot-high palisades. The rounds were fired against no particular target and seemed to Colonel Hamilton a waste of powder. Hamilton knew Clark was no fool and not a man to waste powder if he had none to waste. He concluded then that the Americans had ample powder, which was what Clark wanted him to conclude.

Throughout the night Clark's men threw up earthworks before the fort. At dawn the defenders opened fire with artillery. Clark's Rangers picked off the gunners, never wasting a shot. By midafternoon Colonel Hamilton had had enough and surrendered.

Clark admired the man for his courage but detested him for buying scalps from Indians. He sent him back to Williamsburg in chains. The man he sent him to was Tom Jefferson, who had now succeeded Patrick Henry as governor of Virginia.

☆

6

Tom Jefferson was elected governor of Virginia June 1, 1779, when he was thirty-six years of age. It was an office which, like many others he was to occupy, he did not seek. It was thrust upon him because of his work with George Wythe, George Mason, Richard Henry Lee and many others in reforming the laws of Virginia. Jefferson was in the forefront of this work. He saw in the Revolution not merely a chance to overthrow the rule of Great Britain, but a unique opportunity to establish in the United States a democracy so just that it would light the way for the rest of the world.

No democracy, he believed, could function unless the people were educated. He did not believe in the rule of an illiterate mob but in the rule of an educated citizenry. For this reason he tried again and again to establish a free schooling system, going all the way from grade school through university. He did not entirely succeed in this, but he paved the way for the eventual success of others.

The actual fighting of the Revolutionary War, he left to others whom he believed far more competent than he. He had courage in plenty but he believed a man should work in the field to which he was best suited. The cavalry charges he led were against cruel laws and crippling statutes which killed the spirit of men quite as certainly as cannon shot killed their bodies. In this area he fought many actions against appalling odds. He was often defeated but he never surrendered.

Before he became governor of Virginia, Jefferson took one step which could have cost him all his popularity. The prisoners taken by the Continental Army after the Battle of Saratoga were sent to Virginia and quartered in Albemarle, only a few miles from Monticello.

They were both German and British and were housed and fed at state expense. Virginia was hard pressed for money. Her finances were in tatters and, as the result of the war and the British blockade by sea, all her trade had ceased. She supplied men and money to the Continental Army. It seemed hard then to have to house and feed several hundred British and German prisoners. A plea was made to Governor Patrick Henry to have the prisoners removed from the

★

state. It was argued that the provisions they consumed were needed for the Continental forces.

Henry and his council were about to order the prisoners sent out of Virginia—where, nobody seemed quite sure—when Jefferson heard of the proposal. He knew the prison camp well. The men had converted the rough barracks in which they were placed into something approaching homes. They had begged for a little ground and laid out vegetable gardens to grow food for themselves. They were peaceable and civil and, if they were sent somewhere else, they would undoubtedly be moved from place to place and many of them would sicken and die.

Jefferson immediately wrote a petition to the governor and council on behalf of the prisoners. No one but the man who wrote the Declaration of Independence would speak for the captured enemy. He argued that the prisoners' health would be jeopardized if they were moved about from place to place. He asked that "humanity should not be kicked out of door in America, and interest only attended to." He pleaded that "It is for the benefit of mankind to mitigate the horrors of war as much as possible." He wrote on behalf of the wretched prisoners with the same fervor he had employed in writing for the people of the thirteen colonies. His plea was successful and the prisoners were allowed to remain at Albemarle. They never forgot his kindness to them.

But then, after he had been elected governor, he had to deal with another kind of prisoner. This was

★
75

Colonel Henry Hamilton, British commander at Detroit, the man who had incited the Indians to wage war on the American settlers, the man who had paid the Indians money for the scalps of men, women and children.

Hamilton, sent by George Rogers Clark, arrived in chains. With him, also in chains, were Philip DeJean, Justice of the Peace for Vincennes, and William Lamothe, captain of volunteers, men who were as bloody as their master in the treatment of settlers. They arrived with a request from Clark that they be "severely dealt with."

Jefferson, the most humanitarian of men, was asked to inflict an inhuman punishment on three of his fellows—to chain them by their arms and legs in a prison cell. He hated the whole concept. It was contrary to his nature. He had been governor of Virginia only two weeks when he was presented with this problem and to solve it he called together his council.

The council reviewed all the crimes against the frontiersmen committed by the three, led by Hamilton. They included not only scalpings but torture and beating of prisoners. When all the evidence was in, the council decided that the three should be put in irons, confined in the dungeons of the public jail, debarred from the use of pen, ink and paper and excluded from all conversation with others—except their keeper.

The council had more than the individual crimes of Hamilton in mind when this decision was taken. Men of the Continental Army, captured by the British, had

★
76

been treated not as prisoners of war but as felons. They were put in prison ships where the greater part of them died of smallpox. They were kept in chains and given only offal to eat. They lived in their own filth, being deprived of any sanitary facilities. The dead were taken off these terrible prison ships every evening and buried in unnamed graves below the high-tide mark.

Jefferson's decision, taken with his council, to keep Hamilton, DeJean and Lamothe in irons raised a storm around him. Sir Guy Carlton, governor of Canada, protested against it and so did General William Phillips, commander of the British prisoners at Charlottesville, who was himself a prisoner of war. They accused Jefferson of a violation of faith and of inhuman conduct.

Jefferson wanted to do what was right. He wrote to Washington and, after outlining the crimes of which Hamilton was guilty, said that if there was anything illegal in the punishment involved they would gladly change it.

Washington consulted with his general officers and wrote back that Hamilton could not "according to the usages of war . . . be subjected to any uncommon severity." He added, however, that "I should not hesitate to withhold from him a thousand privileges I might allow to common prisoners."

Jefferson reviewed the case again with his council and decided to publish all the crimes of which Hamilton and his lieutenants were guilty. He would take the

★
77

chains off Hamilton and the other two and allow them a reasonable amount of liberty in return for their parole not to attempt to escape or plot against their captors.

But Hamilton was a hard and proud man. He was brilliant, brave, cruel, unbending and completely contemptuous of the Americans. He refused to give his parole. In particular, he refused to promise not to say anything to the prejudice of the United States. He wanted, he said, "freedom of speech."

Jefferson put him back in jail and wrote Washington that, as far as he was concerned, Hamilton was in jail of his own free will. He could get out if he would sign the same parole that everybody else signed.

The British, in the meantime, demanding Hamilton's release, had stated that unless Hamilton was freed of his chains, they would put chains on all American officers in their prisons.

On getting this news, Jefferson came very close to losing his temper. He said it was lucky for Hamilton that his fate had been decided before the threat was made, otherwise things might have gone even worse for him. He would not, he declared, be bullied by British threats and he defied the British to carry them out. There were far more British officers in American custody than American officers in British custody. If it came to chaining prisoners, the British would lose heavily, he said.

Many attempts were made to have Hamilton freed

in an exchange of prisoners. But Jefferson would not free him. The man was savagely hostile to Americans. To free him would be to have him return again to Detroit, arouse the Indians once more and start his bloody scalping campaigns in the territory that George Rogers Clark had conquered for the new nation. So Jefferson kept Hamilton in prison. In doing so, he ensured the new frontier and helped his friend George Rogers Clark.

Up to this point most of the campaigns of the war had been fought in the northern states and Virginia had not been invaded by the King's troops. But now the tide of war swung from the North to the South. Jefferson, a man of peace and reason, was brought directly into the problem of waging war.

He had no experience in the field of war; this was probably the only area in which he had done no reading. His duty, as he saw it, was to supply Washington with all the men and materials that Virginia could produce. He had also the job of maintaining a force of militia in Virginia for the defense of the state should it be invaded. But he soon discovered that there were not enough men, not enough arms, not enough clothing, not enough food, not enough ammunition to defend the state and supply Washington.

When Charleston fell to the British, it seemed highly likely that Virginia would be invaded from the South and the legislature voted to give Jefferson emergency powers to defend the state. He was authorized

★

to raise twenty thousand militiamen and to appropriate cattle, linen for tents, horses, wagons, boats and crews or whatever was necessary to supply them.

But Jefferson soon found that he had, in effect, been voted nothing. He could raise the militiamen on paper but not in the field. There were no supplies to be found for those who answered the call to serve the state. He sent the men in companies to different commanders only to have the commanders ask him not to send men unless they were equipped. General Gates wrote him that forty men had arrived at his camp at Hillsboro, North Carolina. They had no equipment and he had no stores for them. He asked Jefferson to send no more men unless they were supplied.

Even when Jefferson was able to raise needed military stores, they arrived spoiled at their destination. He sent three hundred cartouche (cartridge) boxes to one commander, but when they arrived the leather sides had been stripped off them to mend shoes. He got six hundred more from the Board of War, but they were unfit for use.

He ordered five hundred axes for Gates's army but the factory was able to turn out only twenty a day. And when he was able to get any quantity of supplies together, there were often no wagons to cart them to where they were needed. All the supplies and men he could get together he sent to General Gates in the South. All were lost at Camden, South Carolina, when Gates was overwhelmingly defeated.

★

After the Battle of Camden the road to Virginia from the South lay open. Jefferson determined to raise more men and arm them as well as he could to block the British invasion. He got some from the western counties—frontiersmen who reckoned fighting was a part of living. But many of the militia raised had never seen a shot fired in anger, were unarmed and improperly clothed and fled from battle in sheer fright.

Virginia was about to learn what the northern states had learned some years before: you can't make a soldier by giving a man a gun and a flag. In Virginia's case there wasn't even a gun to give him. Guns, tents, cartridge boxes, food wagons had been sent without stint to what Tom Jefferson called the "grand army," (that is, the Continental Army) and, in her hour of agony, Virginia had little or nothing with which to defend herself.

Tom Jefferson, as commander-in-chief of Virginia, had no standing army, no navy, no military department, no experienced quartermaster to gather stores and see to their dispatch, no system other than the civil government sending out calls for the militia. He inherited a defenseless state which was now to be threatened on three fronts. It was to be attacked from the sea by Benedict Arnold, who had now gone over to Britain. It was to be attacked from the south by Cornwallis. And it was to be constantly menaced from the west by the Tories (those who sympathized with the British cause) and Indians in the British pay.

★

Without military experience, he had to try to fight a three-front war in a state where communications were of the poorest.

He did his best. He was very much alone, for the great men who were his friends were far away. But eventually help came to him. When he had been governor six months, a young Virginian, James Monroe, who was then only twenty-one years of age, called on him. Monroe wanted to study law, he said, and asked Jefferson to supervise his studies.

It was a curious request in the middle of a war. But Monroe had already served in the Continental Army. He had been present at the Battles of Harlem Heights, White Plains, Trenton, Brandywine, Germantown and Monmouth. He had been wounded at Trenton.

"You wish to study law," said Jefferson, "and I have a desperate need to study soldiering. Perhaps we can help each other." James Monroe had a quick mind and an active curiosity. He undertook to teach Jefferson all he knew of the handling and training and supplying of troops and Jefferson undertook to guide his studies in law.

Jefferson set up a communications system with the Continental Army to the south, standing between Virginia and the Redcoats under Cornwallis. He posted riders every forty miles along the road and dispatched Monroe to General Greene's headquarters to send him news. Greene had replaced Gates after the defeat at Camden. Monroe, his saddlebags stuffed with law books, went off to be Jefferson's eyes on the southern front.

From the north, where Washington was holding the Continental Army together in a watch in New York, Jefferson got frequent reports from the commander-in-chief. Washington warned him whenever a large number of British ships left the New York waters. Whenever he received such a warning, Jefferson had to decide whether to call out the militia or gamble that the ships were not headed for Virginia. If he called out the militia on too many false alarms, the day would eventually come when they would refuse to answer a call. If he failed to call the militia when an invasion actually took place, he would be forever disgraced.

It was no easy task to summon the militia. Virginia was a big state with a poor system of roads. To get messengers to the lieutenants telling them to collect men took days. For the lieutenants to comply with the request took days more. Even a Napoleon could hardly have defended Virginia. But that was the task given to Tom Jefferson.

Washington, knowing Jefferson's situation, sent Baron von Steuben to command the Continental forces in Virginia—such as they were. Jefferson was enormously relieved to have a military expert in the state, for von Steuben was the man who had trained the Continental Army during the terrible winter at Valley Forge. He had served under Frederick the Great and,

★

when he arrived, Tom Jefferson handed over to him command of the militia as well as the Continental forces in Virginia.

The first blow fell in the autumn of 1780 before Von Steuben had arrived. On September 11 Washington wrote Jefferson that a large number of British were leaving New York on transports bound either for Virginia or Carolina. He advised Jefferson to remove any war stores from the neighborhood of navigable rivers where the enemy could get at them.

But Jefferson was helpless to do anything of the sort. He did not know where the blow would fall. Virginia had many rivers and her stores had necessarily to be kept on their banks for the rivers were the only reliable routes through the state. He warned the county lieutenants of the news and waited for more information. When the information came, it was too late.

On the morning of October 20 a huge British fleet, estimated at over fifty ships, put into Hampton Roads at the mouth of the James River. A thousand infantrymen supported by a hundred cavalry were landed. They took over the countryside, rounded up all the stores they could find, went where they pleased, and there was no organized militia to oppose them.

Jefferson tried to organize a body of militia but the task was hopeless. "Of the troops we shall raise, there is not a single man who ever saw the face of an enemy," he wrote to Washington.

The British force, under the command of General Alexander Leslie, did what it pleased for a month on the lower reaches of the James and then departed. They had come in the hope of linking up with Cornwallis who was expected to push north from Carolina. When he did not appear, they left.

When they had gone, Jefferson tried to get the legislature to approve a standing army for Virginia. He did not trust the militia. But the legislature did not act. Jefferson sent to the members a letter from Baron von Steuben, who had arrived in the state, on the condition of the men from Virginia who had been sent to join the Continental Army. They were for the most part either old men or young boys and many of them were ill. Von Steuben could not take care of them nor turn them into soldiers and so was sending them back again. The legislature was unmoved. Jefferson did not have power, as governor, to authorize the raising of a standing army for Virginia. Since the legislature would not vote to have this done, he had to do the best he could with the militia.

New Year's Eve, 1780, fell on a Sunday. That morning Tom Jefferson was up early as usual and sat down to breakfast very worried about his wife Martha. She had given birth to a daughter on November 3 during Leslie's invasion. The baby, christened Lucy Elizabeth, was sickly and his wife was not well either. Jefferson breakfasted alone, attended by his servant Jupiter and oppressed by troubles private and public. He ate mechanically, scarcely noticing what dish was put before him, and when he had all but finished there was a heavy knock at the front door of the house. Jupi-

★

85

ter left the dining room silently, exchanged a few words with a man in the hall and came back with an envelope which he handed to Jefferson.

Jefferson took it, glanced at the envelope and looked up at Jupiter, puzzled. "This is not for me," he said. "It is for General Nelson." General Thomas Nelson was Commander of the Virginia militia under Jefferson. Jefferson called in the messenger. "Who does this come from?" he asked.

"Mr. Jacob Wray of Hampton."

"Do you know what it is about?"

"Ships," said the messenger. "There are some ships off Willoughby's Point. . . ." Jefferson didn't wait to hear more. He tore open the envelope and there it was —a second British invasion. Twenty-seven ships had been sighted off Willoughby's Point. They showed no colors. The writer did not know whether they were French or British, but they looked as though they were coming up the James River to land men.

Jefferson sent for Nelson and told him to go to the mouth of the James and take control there. He sent for Captain James Maxwell, who was commissioner of Virginia's largely imaginary navy, and told him to accompany Nelson and see what he could do to prevent a landing. He wrote to Baron von Steuben asking for his help. Then he waited, for without further news there was nothing more he could do.

Two days went by without a word. Then came a letter from Nathanael Burwell, county lieutenant of James City. The fleet, Burwell wrote, consisted of

★

86

twenty-one transports and two men-of-war. There were a number of flat-bottomed boats astern of the ships and they were full of men. It was headed up the river with the wind fair. Burwell had only two hundred men under his command and could do nothing to prevent the invasion. The ships were under the command of General Arnold.

Jefferson informed the House of Delegates of the news and said that the ships were going up the river as fast as horsemen, carrying news of them, could ride along the banks. The House met and decided that the militia must be called up. To speed the call the delegates adjourned the meeting and, leaping on their horses, rode as hard as they could to their own counties to rally the men.

There was a race now between horsemen and ships, the ships plunging steadily up the river, all sails drawing, raising a white bow wave before them, the horsemen clattering at a gallop to Henrici, Hanover, Goochland, Fluvanna, Albemarle and Amherst counties to call out the militia.

The men were to assemble at Richmond and Petersburg on the Appomattox, according to the counties they came from. They were to come under their own officers and bring their own arms. But when they arrived, they were to put themselves under the command of field officers who would be waiting for them.

This was Baron von Steuben's idea. He'd seen enough of militia officered by country gentlemen with no battle experience. He wanted men who had smelled

★

87

powder in command and Jefferson, knowing the touchiness of the Virginians, wrote to the county lieutenants explaining this need and asking them to cooperate.

The gathering of the militia was slow and meanwhile the British ships pushed on up the river. There was a small battery at a narrow strait of the river called Hoods and as the ships came into range the battery opened fire. The British landed a party and took the battery which was defended by only fifty men. The river road to Richmond, the capital of Virginia, now lay open to them.

Jefferson left his desk and took to the field. He rode to Westham, a few miles to the north of Richmond, to supervise the removal of stores to the other side of the river where the enemy would not look for them. He sent his wife and children to safety. He worked at moving the stores until late at night and joined his wife at Tuckahoe, where they had been sent at one in the morning. He got a few hours' rest and then sent his family to Fine Creek, an estate about twenty miles above Richmond where they would be safe.

When they were on their way, he joined Colonel John Nicholas of the local militia, crossed over the James River and supervised the removal of arms and other stores to safety.

He found a large supply of guns and ammunition lying in the open. They had been taken from Richmond and just dumped and were within easy range of the British guns. He had them removed and then

★

rode on to the village of Manchester, which lay on the south bank of the James River opposite Richmond.

When he got there he knew that he was too late. The British ships had won the race with the horsemen and the militia. The British had landed infantry and cavalry at Westover, farther down the river, marched to Richmond, set fire to a foundry there, a boring mill and the powder magazine. Across the James River Jefferson could see the smoke pouring up from the burning buildings; he caught an occasional glimpse of a Redcoat as files of soldiers moved along the water-front streets. There was no one to oppose them. Despite all his efforts to call up the militia, only about two hundred were available for the defense of Richmond and they faced a force of 1,500 infantry and from fifty to a hundred cavalry.

Jefferson had been up and in the saddle since before dawn. It was now late in the afternoon. He was anxious to get in touch with Baron von Steuben and set out for a place called Chetwoods to meet him there. But his horse suddenly collapsed under him from exhaustion. Jefferson took off the saddle and bridle and walked to the nearest farm where he found an unbroken colt. He borrowed it from the farmer, saddled it and went on, sick at heart over the inabilty of his beloved Virginia to defend herself from the enemy.

Baron von Steuben was not the mildest tempered of men, but he showed remarkable patience during the British invasion of Richmond. Munitions, taken from

★

storehouses to get them out of the hands of the British, had been hidden without any record of the hiding place and nobody could find them later. Flints were in one place and gunlocks in another and nobody knew exactly where. Von Steuben got men without guns and then he got guns without locks, by which time the men had gone home in disgust.

Still he bore up. Jefferson in a letter asked him what he needed and von Steuben eventually found Jefferson and the governor's council and he told them. He needed four thousand militiamen, armed. That was what he needed. But, though it might be possible to get four thousand militiamen together, it was quite impossible to arm them. He had to make do with what could be scraped together.

Then on January 9, 1781, while Jefferson was trying to restore some order in Richmond after the British left the town, a big-boned, red-haired man in deerskins called on him.

"I figured you might need a little help, Mr. Jefferson," he said. "So I came."

It was George Rogers Clark. For a moment Tom Jefferson could hardly say a word. Then he called for a horse and sent Clark to Baron von Steuben with a note reading, "Colonel Clark of Kaskaskia, having heard of the situation of things, has come to me this morning. I send him to you, supposing you must be in want of officers."

The American frontiersman and the Prussian general sat down together to plan one blow at the enemy.

★

The place they decided to deliver it was at Hoods, the narrow strait through which the British ships must pass when they withdrew down the river. There had been a small battery at this point which the British had raided when they came upstream. It had been impossible to remount the guns, but Von Steuben pointed out that this was something the British didn't know.

"Give me some men and I will set a trap for them," said Clark. He was given three hundred riflemen and thirty horsemen. He put a small company of riflemen as a picket on the point of land at Hoods and hid the rest in low brush to the rear. When the British ships came off Hoods, they stopped and landed troops from eighteen boats to attack what they thought was a battery ready to fire on the ships. They met the picket line, which fired off a few rounds and retreated.

Cheering, the British charged right into the ambush Clark had set for them. The militia opened fire and seventeen Redcoats were killed and as many wounded. But the British rallied and came on with the bayonet. The militia broke and fled, for they had no bayonets, and that was the end of the engagement.

It was the only real engagement of the invasion. The British retreated to the head of the river where Arnold had established headquarters at Portsmouth.

Tom Jefferson loathed Benedict Arnold. It was humiliating to have Virginia invaded and be so helpless, but it was even more humiliating that the invasion should be headed by a man who had betrayed his

★

country. He wrote to General John Muhlenberg, who was on von Steuben's staff, suggesting a plan to capture Arnold, using a few men like George Rogers Clark from the frontier.

He believed frontiersmen could get into Arnold's camp and seize the traitor and he was prepared to offer a reward of five thousand guineas for the capture. But before such a plot could be perfected, Washington sent a small force to the aid of his native Virginia. At the head of it was a young man whom Jefferson was to come to love—the Marquis de Lafayette.

☆

7

Marie Joseph Paul Yves Roch Gilbert du Motier, Marquis de Lafayette was not quite twenty-four years of age when he led an army of scarcely a thousand men into Virginia to the succor of the state and Thomas Jefferson.

He had been nineteen and a captain of dragoons in the French Guards when he heard the news of the Declaration of Independence and his heart went out immediately to the Americans. It was a curious love affair this—between a French nobleman with an immense fortune and American republicans to whom nobility was detestable. But Lafayette was at heart a republican himself and the fact that he had inherited an ancient title and a vast estate did not prevent him for a moment from deciding then and there to join the American cause.

In December 1776 he obtained from Silas Deane, one of the American agents in Paris, a letter which would give him, he thought, the rank of major general in the Continental Army. He had hardly received this paper before news of the defeat of Washington's army in the battle to hold New York City reached France. Lafayette's friends begged him to remain in France. The American cause, they assured him, was lost. Even Ben Franklin, who had recently arrived in Paris, tried to persuade Lafayette to give up the idea of joining Washington's stricken army.

But Lafayette started fitting out a ship in Bordeaux to take him to America. The British ambassador managed to have the ship seized to prevent Lafayette's sailing. Lafayette was detained in custody. The ship was sent to Spain. Lafayette escaped in disguise, joined the ship and sailed. He landed in Georgetown, South Carolina, and hurried to Philadelphia. The only English he spoke was what he had learned on crossing the Atlantic from the sailors on board the ship.

As soon as he reached Philadelphia, Lafayette presented himself to Congress with Silas Deane's letter. Congress was embarrassed. There were plenty of Americans who had been refused the rank of major general and who had more claim to it than this boyish French nobleman. And yet a high rank had been promised him by Silas Deane and on this promise he had hurried from France at his own expense to help the cause.

Lafayette understood the difficulty. In fumbling

★

English he told the members of the Congress that rank did not matter. He would serve as a simple volunteer without rank if they would accept him. Congress was so impressed with his zeal that the members decided to give him the rank of major general in any case, and sent him to Washington. Six weeks later Lafayette took part in the Battle of Brandywine and was wounded on the field. He fought at the battles of Barren Hill and of Monmouth, and now here he was leading a handful of Continental troops to the aid of Virginia.

When he met Jefferson, he confessed that he had one deep fear.

"Of what are you afraid?" asked Jefferson.

"Myself, sir," said Lafayette. "I have to watch myself very carefully. I have too much—how you say?—enthusiasm. I want to attack. But I cannot attack for we are outnumbered seven to one or more and we will certainly be beaten. I am in a curious position, Your Excellency. If I attack, we lose. If I retreat, people will say all is lost. The only thing to do is to skirmish until the odds are better."

Lafayette had a gaiety in the face of disaster that was infectious. Even the news of his coming cheered Jefferson immensely and he started to work again to raise more militia, more volunteers for the Continental Army, more guns and ammunition. But before Lafayette arrived, the British had struck another blow at all-but-defenseless Virginia.

Arnold, after his first raid, had withdrawn to Ports-

★

95

mouth and there he was joined by Major General William Phillips, who had been sent with 2,600 reinforcements to take over command from Arnold.

Phillips had been one of the British prisoners for whom Jefferson had interceded with Patrick Henry to prevent their being moved from place to place. He was often a guest at Monticello in the days before Tom Jefferson became governor. Jefferson thought so highly of him that when he became governor, he wrote Phillips a letter of farewell, saying he would miss his company. And now Phillips, freed in an exchange of prisoners, was back again at the head of an invading army.

On April 18, 1781 Arnold, on Phillips' instructions, put 2,500 men on board ships at Portsmouth and sent them up the James River. They landed on the south bank and marched toward Petersburg. There General Muhlenberg, who before the war had been a parson, blocked his path with one thousand militia who had never before been in battle.

This time the militia gave a good account of themselves. They opened fire with guns charged with grapeshot but they were outnumbered and outflanked and finally had to withdraw. There was no panicky flight but a withdrawal in good order. Virginia was learning about war at first hand, and men's nerves were steadier.

Muhlenberg led his men back across the Appomattox and Petersburg was looted by the Redcoats. The invaders pushed on up the river, warehouses going up in smoke and scattered actions being fought wherever the outnumbered militia could make a stand. Arnold led one branch of the British invasion and Phillips another and the two met at Manchester on the south bank of the James River opposite Richmond.

It was then that Lafayette, coming down from the north, reached Richmond and the two armies faced each other across the river. There was a curious stunned silence as they faced each other across the James. Not a shot was fired. Both sides seemed to sense that a critical stage in the war had been reached. Phillips and Arnold, dealing only with militia, had been able to do what they wished in Virginia. And now here were Continental veterans led by a brilliant officer. The tide was about to turn.

The British did make one attempt to send a small party across the river to discover the strength of Lafayette's forces. Six hundred of them, under Arnold's command, went over to the Richmond side but they were charged by a patrol of sixteen cavalry and fled. The arrival of Lafayette seemed to have broken the nerve of the British troops.

As soon as he had reached Richmond, Lafayette sent a message to Baron von Steuben to join him there. He called on Jefferson, who had remained in the capital, to present his compliments.

"My plan, Your Excellency," he said, "is to hold Richmond and I delight in doing it for it is the capital city of that state which first boldly spoke out for independence."

★

The genuine admiration in Lafayette's voice as he said this took Jefferson by surprise. He looked keenly at the young Frenchman to see whether this was a court speech, a piece of mere flattery, or sincerely given. But it was plain that Lafayette meant every word. The young nobleman had looked forward immensely to meeting the man who had written the Declaration of Independence. It was the spirit of that Declaration that had brought Lafayette to America as a volunteer. Jefferson looked weary and older than his years. Lafayette did not know that Jefferson's little daughter Elizabeth had died just two weeks before.

"I am more happy than I can say that you have come to our aid," Jefferson said. "I am not a soldier. I . . ."

"Many of us are soldiers, Your Excellency," said Lafayette quietly. "There is only one Jefferson."

At the time of his meeting with Lafayette, Jefferson had only one more month to serve as governor of Virginia. He had served two full terms of a year each and the state constitution forbade him to retain office beyond June 1 of 1781. But no one had been elected to replace him. Nobody was anxious to be governor with Virginia in such a state. Jefferson's lieutenant governor, Dudley Digges, instead resigned. The members of the legislature could not be called together because of the turmoil the state was in and because there was no safe place where they could meet. It was becoming increasingly hard for Jefferson to get the members of his council together for advice. He was, as was so often the case, utterly alone in his trial.

Then came another blow. Cornwallis, who had been held at bay in North Carolina, now plunged north to link up with General Phillips and Arnold. Lafayette was likely to be caught between the two British armies. He had received news that General Anthony Wayne was hurrying to his aid, but Wayne was delayed.

There was nothing for Lafayette to do but to retreat to prevent the British getting between him and Wayne.

Cornwallis was sure that he had Lafayette trapped and to Jefferson it seemed the Frenchman could not escape. With only a few days more in office, he once more wrote to the county lieutenants asking for men for Lafayette.

But Virginians, still not thoroughly aroused to war, resisted turning over their horses to provide a much-needed cavalry.

The British seized what horses they wanted. Jefferson had no such power and when he got the power, it came too late. Two British armies were already in the state and the time to raise and train an efficient cavalry force had long passed.

Almost in despair, with the whole problem of organizing the defense thrust into his hands, Jefferson wrote to Washington. He suggested that Washington himself come to Virginia to restore public confidence.

★

If Washington came, Jefferson said, the difficulty would be to keep men out of the army. Richard Henry Lee also wrote Washington, asking him to come to Virginia. But Washington believed that the war would be won or lost in New York and not Virginia and so he refused to leave the Hudson.

Jefferson's appeal to Washington was made on May 28, 1781. He had only three more days to serve as governor. The House of Delegates finally met in Charlottesville, three miles from Monticello, and on May 30 passed a resolution that on the following Saturday, June 2, they would elect a new governor. But they did not get around to the election until June 12. The new governor was General Thomas Nelson, who had commanded the state militia under Jefferson. Jefferson had recommended him as his successor.

When his term as governor was over Jefferson returned home. He was worn out and he needed desperately to rest. He needed his own house and his own family around him and he was sick with the frustration he had endured as a wartime governor, with his inability, whatever his efforts, to stem the British invasion of Virginia. He had done everything he could to the best of his ability and yet the failure weighed heavily on him.

It was the blackest period of his life to date and the five years which had passed since the writing of the Declaration of Independence seemed to him five centuries.

He returned to Monticello weary, nervously ex-

★

hausted and so troubled he could scarcely sleep at night. What good was it to write of independence if he could not sustain it in the field against the enemy?

When Martha met him she cried, looking at his haggard face, "Tom, you must rest!"

He stared at her as if he did not understand the meaning of the words.

Patsy eyed him gravely. "Papa," she said, "there are some big peaches in the orchard and lots of cherries."

Then, for the first time in two years, a little ease came to him. Things were still growing at Monticello. All would be well in the end.

8

Charlottesville being only a few miles away, several members of the Virginia legislature, including the Speaker of the House, were staying at Monticello. There were not enough accommodations in Charlottesville for the delegates and, to get together sufficient to conduct the business of the state (including electing a successor as governor), Jefferson put up as many as he could in his own home.

He had ceased to be governor June 1. There was now a strong movement among the delegates to appoint a dictator in the state instead of a governor. Even Patrick Henry believed that only a dictator could save Virginia. But Jefferson was mortified and angered at the thought.

"You cannot secure liberty by a resort to tyranny," he cried.

Eventually he persuaded the delegates to elect Thomas Nelson his successor. This would combine in the office of governor the civil and military power of the state, for Nelson was commander of the Virginia militia. But Nelson was not given dictatorial powers.

Meanwhile the British were ravaging the country from Richmond and Lord Cornwallis, certain that victory was within his grasp, was planning to send some important captives back to London. Most important among them was to be Thomas Jefferson, author of the Declaration of Independence. Another was Richard Henry Lee, who had introduced the resolution for independence into the Continental Congress. Another was Patrick Henry, whose famous speech with the ringing phrase "Give me liberty or give me death" had rallied the country six years before. All these were either at Monticello or at Charlottesville. To capture them, Cornwallis sent his "hunting leopard," Lieutenant Colonel Banastre Tarleton, to raid Charlottesville and Monticello.

Tarleton was a man who was both feared and hated. He was a brilliant, dashing cavalry leader of high courage. He had also slaughtered a great number of Americans who had surrendered to him after being assured that he would spare their lives. Therefore in the Revolutionary War massacre of men who had already surrendered was called "Tarleton's Quarter."

Tarleton's raid to seize Jefferson, Lee, Henry and others was kept completely secret even from the 180 dragoons and seventy mounted infantrymen who were

★

to take part in it. He left Richmond headed up the Rivanna River in what looked like an ordinary expedition to seize and burn American property. He rode hard and did not stop until he reached the Cuckoo Tavern in Louisa County, forty miles in a direct line from Charlottesville. Here the men dismounted to rest their sweating, hard-breathing horses and here Captain Jack Jouett of the Virginia militia saw them.

Jack Jouett was a giant of a man. He stood six feet four and weighed two hundred pounds. He knew horses and he knew cavalry and he knew that horses were not ridden hard until late in the evening without there being a very urgent reason.

He dared not question the troopers in the tavern about their mission. Nor did he dare mix with them to pick up a chance remark. What military prize, he wondered, lay in this quiet part of the country—a prize so important that over two hundred men on excellent horses had been sent to seize it? There could be only one answer: Tom Jefferson, whose home at Monticello lay up the Rivanna River. Tarleton, the "hunting leopard," was out to seize Tom Jefferson and as many men of the Virginia legislature as he could. There could be no other reason for this expedition.

It was ten o'clock at night when Jouett came to this conclusion. He knew exactly what he had to do. His own home was nearby. He hurried there and mounted a big hunter and set off on a forty-mile ride to warn Jefferson. He dared not take the river road along the banks of the Rivanna to Monticello. He had to go

★

through the back country, through tangles of brush and low-branching trees, guided by his own knowledge of the country and an occasional glimpse through the treetops of the stars.

He rode through the night, not sparing his horse. Branches slashed at his face as he plunged through the trees, ripping the skin. He galloped on, up hills and through gullies, and at four-thirty in the morning plunged up the little mountain at whose top stood Monticello. The whole house was in darkness and peace, only its roof and the pillars before it gleaming softly in the moonlight.

Jouett jumped off his hunter and went up the steps before the enormous front door two at a time and knocked on the door with his riding crop. In a few minutes the door was opened and he shouted to the trembling servants to rouse Mr. Jefferson for Tarleton was coming with a body of troopers to capture him.

Jefferson himself appeared at the door and Jouett repeated his message. Jefferson was quite calm.

"Do you think we have much time?" he asked.

"I cannot say, sir," said Jouett. "But if they do not stop on their way, they will be here any minute."

"I think there is at least time to offer you a glass of wine and thank you," said Jefferson and poured a drink of his finest Madeira for Jouett. Jouett drank the Madeira and then set off to Charlottesville to warn the others, including Patrick Henry. He reached Charlottesville in less than half an hour and warned Henry and the others.

★

Jefferson arranged for Martha and his two daughters to be taken by carriage to Enniscorthy, about fourteen miles away, where they would be safe.

While he was making these arrangements, Captain Christopher Hudson of the militia arrived to say that the troopers were already at the foot of the mountain and he must leave immediately.

The Jefferson family went off but Jefferson, who had had to wait for a horse to be shoed, tied the horse at a point on the road between Monticello and nearby Carter's Mountain. He walked up the mountain with a telescope. From the top he could get a view of Charlottesville and, looking through the telescope, could see no troopers in the streets of the little town.

He decided then that he still had time and started back toward Monticello for he was anxious about some papers he had left in his study. As he walked to his horse, he noticed that he had dropped a light sword and returned to pick it up. On top of the mountain again, he took out his telescope once more for a look at Charlottesville. He was astonished to see the green coats of Tarleton's mounted infantrymen swarming in the streets.

There was no time now to get his papers. He jumped on his horse and galloped off into the woods after his family. Actually, the British had already reached Monticello when Jefferson at last decided it was time to escape.

Tarleton didn't come to Monticello himself. He sent

some troopers there under the command of a Captain McLeod. He gave strict instructions to McLeod about the mansion. Nothing was to be taken away or damaged. When McLeod arrived there, he asked the servant for the keys to Jefferson's study. When he got them, he locked the door to ensure that nothing was disturbed by his troopers.

Jefferson's servants did not of course know that their master's possessions were to be spared. One of his slaves, Martin, was passing Jefferson's silver to another, Caesar, through a trapdoor leading to the cellar when the troopers arrived. Martin slammed the door shut on Caesar and Caesar stayed there eighteen hours in silence until the raiders had gone.

Cornwallis meanwhile had moved up to Elk Hill, another house of Jefferson's at the junction of the Rivanna and Fluvanna rivers. In contrast to Tarleton's behavior, Cornwallis let his men burn the barn, destroy the crops and even cut the throats of young colts. Thirty Negro slaves were carried off. When Jefferson learned that his slaves had been taken away, he went white with indignation—even though he rarely got angry.

"If he did this to set them free and provide for them, I would have helped him," he said. "But he did it only to let them sicken and die." As soon as he could, after the surrender at Yorktown, Jefferson set out to look for his slaves. He found only two alive. The rest had died of neglect and smallpox.

★

After his escape, Jefferson rejoined his family and he had to tell Patsy over and over again about his adventures. She was enormously proud of her father.

"My daddy went back for his sword to fight all those troopers," she told everybody. Even her truth-loving father could not get her to accept another version.

When he got back to Monticello with his family, news of another attack on him reached Thomas Jefferson. A friend of his in the legislature sent word that a motion was to be introduced at the next meeting asking for an inquiry into the conduct of "the Executive" during his last twelve months in office. The Executive, of course, meant both Jefferson and his council, but Jefferson knew that the inquiry was directed at him. The resolution was sponsored by George Nicholas, a young member of the House of Delegates and the eldest son of Robert Carter Nicholas who had been one of Jefferson's friends in happier days.

Jefferson knew that young George Nicholas had not initiated this resolution himself. He was being used as a tool by others. He suspected, though he was never able to prove the suspicion, that Patrick Henry was behind the resolution. He was outraged and saddened. He had admired Patrick Henry deeply. He, Patrick Henry, Richard Lee and George Wythe had been the four who had pushed the old colonial legislature of Virginia toward boldness and independence. He had supported Patrick Henry loyally when Henry was governor of the state. Now this cloud passed between the two friends. Although Jefferson continued to speak only good of Patrick Henry, there was a coldness between the two from that time on.

As soon as he received news of the resolution, Jefferson wrote to George Nicholas. "I am informed that a resolution on your motion passed the House of Delegates requiring me to render account of some part of my administration without specifying the act to be accounted for," he said, and demanded to be told exactly what charges were laid against him or exactly what part of his conduct needed investigation.

Nicholas replied that there was no particular instance of misconduct in mind. People who were entrusted with an administration ought to be ready to give an account of any part of it. The young delegate then defended himself.

"You consider me in a wrong point of view when you speak of me as an accuser," he wrote. "As a freeman and the representative of freemen, I consider it as both my right and my duty to call upon the Executive to account for our numberless miscarriages and losses so far as they were concerned in or might have prevented them. . . . I had no private pique to gratify. . . ."

The letter went on, however, to specify certain aspects of Jefferson's second term as governor that Nicholas thought needed explanation. Among them were:

The total want of opposition to Arnold on his first expedition.

★

The dissolution of a considerable body of militia on our southern frontier at the time of Greene's retreat for want of orders from the executive.

The want of timely orders to the counties of Amherst, Augusta, etc., after the adjournment of the Assembly from Richmond.

The great loss that the country has sustained in arms, etc., exclusive of those destroyed by the enemy.

The rejection of an offer made by Cole Campbell, Christian and McDowell to raise regiments for the southern services.

So the charges went on, always containing the imputation that Thomas Jefferson had been so lax in his efforts to defend Virginia that the state had been mercilessly pillaged by the enemy. Virginians felt keenly the invasion of their state, the more so because Arnold had led one of the invading fleets. They were looking for a scapegoat and Jefferson was a wonderful target —Jefferson who, with his revision of the laws, had destroyed the hold of the older families on Virginia.

Rumors accusing Tom Jefferson of conduct close to treasonous and even cowardice spread throughout the thirteen colonies, as those who hated his reforms got busy with loose pens and loose tongues. Nothing that had ever happened to Jefferson hurt him so deeply as this, for he loved Virginia as he loved the cause of independence and as he hated tyranny.

Alone he started to prepare his defense. He sent messengers to the county lieutenants asking them for statements on his many efforts to call out and equip the militia. He was not afraid of the charges but only terribly hurt by them because they were dishonorable and they sought to dishonor him, a man who had always put honor above everything.

He had many friends, however. Among them were Edmund Pendleton, who had worked with him in the early days of the rebellion against the King's tyranny, and James Madison, whom he had befriended when they first met only a few years before in the Virginia House of Delegates.

Without a word from Jefferson, his allies decided to help him. John Blair, one of the Virginia delegates to the Continental Congress, had resigned and John Page, Jefferson's boyhood friend, John Banister and other friends of Jefferson were appointed to a committee to name a substitute. They selected Thomas Jefferson so that, while Jefferson faced investigation for his conduct as governor of Virginia, he was appointed by the state of Virginia to be the state's delegate to the Continental Congress.

He accepted the appointment with gratitude but remained in Virginia to prepare his defense.

The charges against him had been leveled in June. It was not until December that there was any hearing on them in the House of Delegates. At the hearing Nicholas, who had framed the original resolution calling for an inquiry, was not present. Patrick Henry, whom Jefferson believed to be behind the charges, did not rise to press the case.

★

111

Indeed everybody seemed thoroughly ashamed of themselves. A committee which had been appointed to frame the charges specifically and receive any evidence supporting them reported to the House that there was nothing in the charges—that they were utterly groundless.

But Jefferson's name had been blackened and he did not welcome this report. He wanted an inquiry held so that item by item and charge by charge he could deal with everything that had been said against him. So that he might appear in the House of Delegates on an equal footing with his accusers, one of the members resigned and Jefferson was appointed in his place.

He rose then in the House, tall, spare and haggard and challenged the delegates to impeach him. It was not sufficient to ask for an inquiry, he stated, to blacken his name before the whole nation, and then to say when the damage to his reputation was done that an inquiry was needless and he was innocent. The House, silent and in an agony of mortification, was forced to listen while Jefferson reviewed the whole of his administration as governor, told in every detail all he had done to save Virginia and demanded in so many words that they be decent enough to try him.

A trial, however, was quite impossible. There were no charges that could be brought. Jefferson had been made the victim of something quite common in eighteenth century politics both in Britain and America—a smear campaign.

When he had done with his defense, member after

member rose to eulogize his work as governor. The members who spoke were deeply moved and sensed the terrible wrong they had done to Jefferson. The House passed a resolution "that the sincere thanks of the General Assembly be given to our former Governor, Thomas Jefferson, Squire, for his impartial, upright, and attentive administration while in office. The Assembly wish in the strongest manner to declare the high opinion which they entertain of Mr. Jefferson's ability, rectitude, and integrity, as Chief Magistrate of this Commonwealth, and mean, by thus publicly avowing their opinion, to obviate and remove all unmerited censure."

The vote on this was unanimous and when it was taken the delegates crowded around Jefferson, shaking his hand and patting his shoulder. He thanked them quietly and left for Monticello. Then he wrote, resigning his seat in the Continental Congress.

He had come to a firm resolve. He would never again take any public office or work in the public service. He wanted only to live as a private citizen with his family, among his books, building his house and carrying out his agricultural experiments.

He wanted the peace and the quiet of his home. The blow that had been struck at him deprived the United States for a while of the services of a man who had won the respect of the world.

☆

9

By 1781 the war was in its fifth year. The alliance with France, patiently forged by John Adams and Ben Franklin, had turned the tide and even King George III, who had already suffered one fit of insanity, had come to the conclusion that Britain could not win. Rumors of peace were in the air, rumors which came strangely to the ears of the British commanders, Clinton in New York and Cornwallis in Virginia.

Their military position, they felt, had never been stronger. Washington's little army on the Hudson was held together purely by the personality of the commander. Unpaid, ill armed, badly clothed and provisioned almost by the grace of God, Washington's Continental Army was incapable of delivering a major blow. His war chest was so low that he was unable to find a few shillings to pay a courier on a horse for carrying a message a distance of a few miles.

In Virginia, Cornwallis, having linked with Phillips, could ravage the land as he wished and the cities of Virginia, along its many rivers, lay under a pall of blue smoke from the thousands of hogsheads of tobacco burned by the Redcoats. Burning tobacco was like burning money, for the only source of cash for the United States of America was Virginia tobacco sold abroad.

Opposing the British in Virginia for a while was "the boy" Lafayette. He danced between the two armies of Cornwallis and Phillips like a gadfly between two bulls, capable of doing no more than irritating them. Down to the succor of Lafayette came "Mad" Anthony Wayne leading a few thousand veterans of the Pennsylvania line. Then came news to Washington's headquarters that the French fleet had left the West Indies and was headed for the Capes of the Chesapeake. Washington, with a prayer that he might not be too late, withdrew from New York and headed south, gathering his French allies on the way and hoping to be able to hem Cornwallis in between the land and the sea at a little hamlet few but Virginians had ever heard of called Yorktown.

But before this mighty change in the military picture took place Adams and Franklin, through the mediation of Russia and Germany, were in touch with the British Court and Parliament, which was anxious for an end to the war.

The Congress was fully aware of these negotiations and voted that four delegates be sent to join Adams in

★

115

negotiating a peace between the United States and Great Britain. One of the men that Congress picked for this work was Tom Jefferson. Samuel Huntington wrote a letter to Jefferson informing him of his appointment and the letter was brought to him at Monticello through Lafayette's headquarters.

This appointment came at the time in June of 1781 when Jefferson had been stunned by the news that an investigation was to be held into his last twelve months as governor of Virginia. Jefferson could not accept the appointment. He discussed it many times with Martha but in the end his high sense of honor forbade him, as he saw it, to run away from the inquiry even in the service of his country. He took almost a month replying to the Congress and turned down the appointment because of "circumstances which take from me the right of accepting so desirable an office."

Lafayette had pleaded with him to go to France and Jefferson dearly wanted to go. French excellence in architecture, in literature and in science appealed enormously to him. But he wrote to Lafayette that all his efforts as governor "have not been such as to give satisfaction to some of my countrymen and it has become necessary for me to remain in the state. . . ."

Others also pleaded with Jefferson to go to France. He was needed there, they said, and they well knew that the charges against him were merely a political smear. But he would not go. He had to defend himself and, even beyond this, he desperately needed to live quietly for a while with his family. Edmund

Randolph, delegate from Virginia to the Continental Congress, wrote bitterly to Jefferson, "I was much distressed . . . to find your irrevocable purpose of sequestering yourself to public life. If you can justify this resolution to yourself, I am confident that you cannot to the world."

Still Jefferson would not go. He needed Monticello. Martha was ill, and he was afraid for her. Indeed something had gone out of Jefferson in his two years as governor. The burning of the land, the slaughtering of horses and cattle, the bloody destruction of all natural things which is warfare at first hand had profoundly shaken him. He needed the quietness and strength of the earth, the peace of the trees to make him whole again.

So at Monticello, while Cornwallis retreated toward Yorktown and the diplomats exchanged their cunning notes concerning peace, Jefferson went on with the building of his house, went for rides with Patsy, laid out more gardens, experimented with fertilizers and turned himself to the whole purpose for which the war had been fought—the decent peaceful living of a free citizen.

Earlier in the year the Marquis François de Barbe-Marbois, who was secretary of the French legation in Philadelphia, had addressed to Jefferson a long letter containing a lot of questions about Virginia. This letter Jefferson, busy with all the affairs of the war, had not had time to answer. Now he turned to answering it and he decided that in his answer he would give all

★
117

the information concerning Virginia that lay at his disposal. He would deal with its plants and its native animals, its geography and its geology, its history, its Indians and its laws. In short, to answer a letter he would write a book. The book would restore his inner strength.

The book became known as *Notes on Virginia*. In it, after painstaking research and a quantity of reading sufficient for a modern college course, Jefferson spoke of such matters as how far the Nansemond River is navigable for a vessel of 250 tons, how long it takes to go by boat from the mouth of the Ohio to the mouth of the Mississippi, the height of the Natural Bridge—a natural arch over a river which Jefferson owned and which he regarded as "the sublimest of Nature's works" —the weights of deer and of hogs, the height of horses and the kinds of turtles and snakes and lizards to be found in the sprawling area then called Virginia. He included notes of maximum and minimum temperatures in Virginia in different seasons of the year, for during all his troubles he had rarely failed to get up at dawn and read his thermometer.

A great French naturalist, the Count de Buffon, had produced a work in which he made the curious claim that the animals of North America were smaller than those of Europe. Jefferson set out to inquire into the truth of this statement and soon had notes on an American hog that weighed one thousand pounds and buffalo that weighed nearly two tons and a buck that weighed an astonishing 3,800 pounds.

★

In his zeal to set the facts right, Jefferson wrote to his friend, George Rogers Clark, out in the Virginia wilderness, asking to be sent specimens of bones of any animals which were unusual. ". . . There is no expense of package or safe transportation which I will not gladly reimburse to procure them safely," Jefferson wrote. "Elk horns of very extraordinary size or anything else uncommon would be very acceptable."

Jefferson had heard of massive bones being discovered in some of the frontier territories—the bones of mastodons and other prehistoric creatures which had once thundered through the tremendous forests of the North American continent. He wanted George Rogers Clark to send him some of these if he should find them. But the frontiersman had his eye on the Indians and his stores of powder and shot and hadn't time to send his friend Tom Jefferson elk horns or mastodon bones.

Jefferson later turned to General John Sullivan of New Hampshire, a big, loyal but quick-tempered Irishman whose criticism of the French had embarrassed the Franco-American alliance during the war. Jefferson asked Sullivan whether he could get him the head and hide of a big moose to show to the Count de Buffon.

Sullivan, who was a man of action, organized a hunting expedition, killed the biggest moose he could find, cut a road through twenty-four miles of snow to get the moose out, stuffed it, added the horns of five great deer and shipped the whole thing to France at a monstrous cost to Tom Jefferson. Sullivan not only wanted

★
119

to oblige his friend, but get a little of his own back from the French who, he felt, had let him down.

Jefferson's *Notes on Virginia* included details on all its rivers and tributaries including as much as was known of the Mississippi, Missouri, Ohio and Illinois.

Jefferson's mind was always traveling to the West. As a little boy his father, Peter Jefferson, had taken him to the top of the small mountain on which Jefferson had built Monticello and he had seen wave after wave of forest and hills rising to the Blue Ridge and Appalachians. It was unexplored territory then and his mind was so captivated by it that from boyhood the West had called him. He was as involved with the mysteries of the Mississippi as he was with the ferries across the James. He knew the men of the frontier, the hungry, questing, unlettered men who did not like cities and the plantations of the rich, and who had gone through the Cumberland Gap to spill into Kentucky and beyond.

When they came back to visit civilized parts, these men called at Monticello with a note from George Rogers Clark and sat in their deerskins on Tom Jefferson's elegant furniture, their moccasined feet resting on his magnificent parquet floor, telling him of the forested reaches of the Ohio, of the shoals and rapids and silences and emptiness. Jefferson listened, humble and entranced.

These men, he always felt, were the American future, and when they described to him the great flights of geese and duck over the western land, the huge stands of timber, the floods to which the rivers were subject, the costumes of the Indians and their language, he drank up every word. In his *Notes on Virginia* he wrote about the Mississippi as if he had himself explored it in one of the clumsy bateaux of the frontiersmen.

"The Mississippi below the mouth of the Missouri is always muddy, and abounding with sandbars which frequently change their place," he wrote. "Its current is so rapid that it never can be stemmed by the force of the wind alone acting on the sails."

With his deerskin visitors at Monticello, Jefferson sailed many a time on the Mississippi and dreamed of the day when it would be an American river.

The man who had defended the rights of the American colonists against the tyranny of England undertook also to defend the character of the red Indian against the prejudices of the white man. The Count de Buffon had described the red Indian as a savage almost without human feeling. Jefferson knew the Indians; they often called on him. He testified to their courage, saying an Indian would defend himself against a host of enemies, choosing death rather than surrender. He stated that the Indians loved their children and even spoiled them, that their friendships were faithful even when they were betrayed.

He quoted the speech of the Mingo chief (known to the whites as Logan) to Lord Dunmore when he was governor of Virginia. "I appeal to any white man," Logan had said, "to say if he ever entered my cabin

★
121

hungry and I gave him no meat; if he ever came cold and naked and I clothed him not." Jefferson said this address was superior to the oratory of Demosthenes and Cicero.

Jefferson's *Notes on Virginia,* begun as an answer to a French marquis, were published later as a book and copies were eagerly sought throughout Europe and are used by scholars to this day. He began the work in June of 1781 and finished in December of the same year.

When the book was finished, Cornwallis had surrendered at Yorktown, the war was over and Jefferson felt his troubles were at an end. He had divorced himself from public affairs, he wanted to do nothing more than devote himself to his family, his music, his horses and science. He spent Christmas with his relatives, the Randolphs, at Tuckahoe and by New Year's Day of 1782 was back at Monticello, looking forward to a future of happiness in his home.

10

For the first few months of the year 1782, Thomas Jefferson lived in complete serenity at Monticello. He was still a member of the House of Delegates of the Virginia legislature, but he did not attend any of the sessions. His fellow delegates, somewhat ashamed of the way they had mistreated him, excused him. Jefferson worked away at the building and planning of Monticello, laying out more and more vegetable and flower plots and reading all he could lay his hands on concerning architecture and horticulture.

The building of the great mansion went slowly. The war had cut off all imports of building materials. Nails were more precious than coins. Glass was not to be obtained, nor paint either. It was possible to go ahead only with some of the brick work, and Tom Jefferson had employed as a bricklayer a deserter from the British army. The man worked well and Jefferson encouraged him in his plans to settle in America.

When spring came, bringing the blossoming of the cherries and the peaches to which Jefferson always looked forward, he cut sprays of flowers and brought them into the house himself. Martha was expecting a baby and was not well. He filled her room with flowers to cheer her up. The baby was born on May 8 and was christened Lucy Elizabeth—the second daughter of that name born to the Jeffersons. The first had died a little while previously.

Martha did not recover from childbirth. She could not leave her bed after the baby was born, and as the weeks went by lost strength daily. The doctor was at Monticello constantly and Jefferson remained by his wife's side day and night. His sister, Martha Carr, came to keep house for him. Jefferson would not leave his wife's side. He would allow no one to feed her but himself. He could coax her to take a spoonful of broth, try to raise her spirits by talking of Patsy and the garden. She fought hard for life but she lost the battle and died on the morning of September 6, 1782.

Jefferson was not with her at the moment of death. He had been by her side for so long that he was in a daze and his sister led him away to the library to rest on a bed he had installed there. She came back a few moments later to tell him that Martha had died. He stared at her in utter disbelief and then toppled to the floor unconscious. For some time he remained in a coma and, when the doctor revived him, he asked

★

everyone to leave him alone and shut the library door. All night long he walked up and down from one end of the library to the other without a pause. For three weeks he would not leave the room nor speak to anyone. He had to be forced to eat. When he was not lying exhausted on the bed, he walked backward and forward over the floor of the library.

It was little Patsy who brought him around. She was just ten years of age. She took over the job of bringing him his food and would not leave the room but would sit quietly with him until he had eaten everything.

She did not bother him with talk but now and then she would mention something she thought important that he would like to hear—like the pumpkins getting bigger and the apples in the orchard that were so big she couldn't get her two hands around them.

She sensed that if he stayed in the library he would die, but if she could get him out he would live. Finally she coaxed him outside to see the leaves turning on the oaks and maples and beeches. She had it all arranged. She took his hand and led him out into the garden. She had had a horse saddled and Tom Jefferson looked at it dumbly and climbed into the saddle. Patsy's pony was saddled too and she mounted also. Without a word, Jefferson headed his hunter over the lonely mountain trails around Monticello, Patsy following on her pony.

When they came back from the ride, Patsy told her aunt, Mrs. Carr, "Papa is going to get well. But we are going to have to ride a lot." She knew that it was in

★

125

the mountains and among the trees that Tom Jefferson would find life again. It was there that the dawn always lay for him.

That evening Thomas Jefferson took his first meal since his wife's death outside the library and in the weeks that followed he gradually overcame his despair and turned to the business of his household.

Patsy was a high-spirited girl and not too careful about her dress. She normally put on whatever clothes came to hand without seeing that the ribbons were ironed and the lace fresh. But during the ordeal of her father's grief she dressed very carefully every day and supervised the servants when they dressed her four-year-old sister, Polly.

Meanwhile, though the war was at an end, the peace had not yet been concluded. Thomas Jefferson's name was constantly mentioned in the Congress as a man who should be sent to Europe to take part in the peace negotiations. James Madison, who was one of the delegates from Virginia to the Congress, was plagued with questions on whether Jefferson would accept the appointment which he had previously turned down.

Madison wondered whether Jefferson would not— now that his wife was dead—want to leave Monticello and his memories for a while and bury himself in public affairs. He hinted to the members of the Congress that this might be so.

Jefferson then was reappointed by a unanimous vote of the Congress as one of the ministers to negotiate the peace with Britain. As soon as the vote was taken,

★

Madison wrote to Edmund Randolph in Richmond asking him to tell Jefferson the news ahead of the official notification. "Tell him that the appointment was unanimous, without a single adverse remark," Madison wrote, for he feared that Jefferson might still be resentful of the public criticism of his term as governor.

Congress was so anxious to secure for the nation the services of Jefferson that when Robert R. Livingston, the Secretary of State, resigned at the same time, it was suggested that if Jefferson did not want to go to France as a peace delegate, he might become Secretary of State of the United States. And so Jefferson was offered two of the highest positions in the national services: Secretary of State or Minister Plenipotentiary to France.

This time he was not long making up his mind; he put his grief firmly aside and replied to the Congress that he would be honored to accept the appointment as one of the ministers for negotiating peace with Britain.

First, however, he took his three little daughters, Patsy, Polly and the baby Lucy, to be inoculated against smallpox. Such inoculation was comparatively new in Jefferson's day and many held that it was harmful. But Jefferson had made his own inquiries and decided that children should be inoculated. He took them to the house of his friend, Colonel Archibald Cary, for the inoculation. When they had recovered, Polly and Lucy were taken to Eppington to another of Jefferson's sisters, Mrs. Elizabeth Eppes.

★

But Tom Jefferson took Patsy with him to Philadelphia. She was his little companion now and he would take her about the world and enjoy with her all the sights that were to be seen. Jefferson and Patsy went to put up at the Indian Queen Tavern in Philadelphia. Patsy had never seen so many people and so many carriages in all her life. Furthermore, she had never seen any shops and she was entranced by the windows with all the marvelous trinkets behind them and demanded to be bought ribbons and brooches and toffee apples and other delights that took her fancy. Jefferson spent the first few days taking Patsy around the city, and the great men of the nation who were all his friends came very near to spoiling the daughter of the man who wrote the Declaration of Independence.

After that Tom Jefferson got seriously to business. He had called on Madison as soon as he arrived in Philadelphia, and told him that he couldn't jump into the middle of the peace negotiations without having at his disposal all the information to date.

"I was aware of that," said Madison with a smile, "and I was prepared for it." He handed Jefferson a portfolio of papers—letters, minutes of meetings, memoranda, estimates on imports and exports and revenues to be derived from them, and so on. Jefferson started his reading and in four days had mastered all these details.

He had expected to be in Philadelphia only ten days before sailing to France. But the French frigate, *Romulus,* on which he was to leave was not ready to go,

★

and ice had forced her to anchor twelve miles down the bay.

Jefferson hired a boat and tried to get through the ice to the frigate. The tide came in, jamming the ice floes up the river, and the boat could neither go backward nor forward. He and Patsy were rescued by a sloop which battered its way through the ice and took them to the *Romulus*.

The *Romulus* was under the command of the Chevalier de Villevine. "Well, sir," said Jefferson when he got aboard, "here I am and perhaps now we can sail."

"Impossible," said the Frenchman. "The British may have surrendered at Yorktown but for them the war is not over. There is a ship of sixty-four guns, four ships of fifty guns, two of forty guns and about twenty-five frigates—all of the British navy and all determined that the *Romulus* will not leave this bay. I trust you will not find me lacking in courage if I suggest that the odds are more than we should face."

"Cannot we ask for a flag of truce to permit us to leave?" asked Jefferson.

"That might detract from the dignity of your country," said the Chevalier. "You do not ask a flag of truce from a nation whose army has recently surrendered to you."

So there it was. Jefferson and Patsy were isolated on a frigate blockaded by the whole British fleet in a freezing bay. The quarters on board were cramped and the food abominable.

The French minister suggested that Jefferson might

★

129

be more comfortable with Patsy if he transferred to the frigate *Guadeloupe*. But she had been ten months under water and only recently raised.

Her timbers were sodden wet and her commander and many of his crew were suffering from rheumatism as a result. Jefferson turned down the offer of transfer to the *Guadeloupe*. He wrote to the Secretary of Foreign Affairs asking for advice and received the reply that, in view of the circumstances, he should not go to France until he received renewed instructions.

Jefferson left the frigate and went to Baltimore, taking lodgings with a Mrs. Langston. Time hung heavy on his hands. Baltimore provided little intellectual exercise or amusements. He took Patsy to a play and walked around the city with her, doing a little shopping and sightseeing, and finally returned to Philadelphia. There he waited until April before the Congress decided that it was not necessary for him to go to France, for the peace negotiations were already well advanced. With considerable relief, Jefferson returned to Monticello.

Back at Monticello spring was in full bloom and Jefferson set out some seeds he had gathered while in Baltimore. There wasn't much he could do about building on the house for materials were still not available. He turned his mind to remodeling the constitution of Virginia with which he had never been satisfied. There were rumors in the air that a convention would be called for this purpose and this time Jefferson wanted to have his say in full. He drew up a

★

complete new constitution for the state and one of the provisions was that a governor should be elected for five years instead of one and should be given the power necessary to execute the laws of the state. He remembered only too well his own experience as governor when all responsibility was laid at his door but without the authority to carry through his various plans.

The whole militia of the state, he urged, should be subject to the governor's directions, though the execution of those orders should be the responsibility of military officers. Jefferson sent a copy of his proposed constitution to Madison in Philadelphia. But the convention he hoped for was never called.

In June of that year Jefferson was elected to the United States Congress, which was to reconvene in November. At this time the Congress was so unpopular with the people that it was almost in hiding. Shortly after Jefferson's election a body of mutinous soldiers demanding their pay had marched on Philadelphia and driven the Congress, which was at its wits' end to find money, in full flight to Princeton.

Jefferson set out for Princeton to take his seat but the Congress, still fleeing from unpaid soldiers, had left. He finally caught up with it in Annapolis where it had taken refuge from the unpaid troops.

It was not the fault of the Congress that the soldiers were unpaid. The Congress had been given the job of running the United States, but without the authority or machinery to raise taxes or enforce its wishes. All the states agreed that the Congress must have the right to tax but each was afraid of contributing more than its neighbor.

Again all the states were agreed that there must be a central government. But they were each determined that that central government should not infringe on what they regarded as their own rights. The problem of states' rights versus federal control is as old as the United States of America.

Jefferson took one problem with him to Annapolis which he was determined to solve. Virginia owned vast areas in the West comprising the whole of modern Kentucky and Ohio. Tom Jefferson had often talked of the future of this area with George Rogers Clark. He had talked a great deal about it with members of the Virginia legislature. He secured the agreement of all concerned to hand over the whole of these vast western provinces of Virginia to the Congress so that they might be developed into separate states and not be held back by Virginia.

With the deed ceding these lands, which were known as the Northwest Territory, went a map in which Jefferson carved out fourteen distinct states in the vast area. He named every one of them and their names were somewhat outlandish and caused chuckles among the Congressmen.

There were names such as Cherronesus, Assenisipia and Pelisipia. These referred to Indian tribes, for Tom Jefferson believed strongly that the Indians should not

★

be ignored and all their treasured traditions forgotten. Other names were a little more acceptable: names such as Michigania and Illinoia. His string of new states extended from west of Lake Superior in the north to the territory which lay between the Mississippi and Georgia in the south. In proposing that they be organized, Jefferson laid down one important principle. The new states should be closed to slavery after 1800.

Congress did not act immediately on this proposal. However, in 1787 it enacted the Northwest Ordinance, which stated that no man born in the Northwest Territory, irrespective of his race, should be a slave. Tom Jefferson had by his vision pushed the area of freedom in the United States of America over thousands of square miles.

While he was attending to all this, he was still concerned about his three little daughters. The two younger ones, Polly and Lucy, he continued to leave with his sister, Mrs. Eppes.

Patsy he now took to Philadelphia where she could be schooled as became a young lady. She was to have dancing lessons and music lessons and drawing lessons. It was very hard for him to part with Patsy. She was a bright and cheerful girl and was able to make him laugh even in the worst of his worries. Her cheerfulness at times disturbed her father, who was quite sure that she would not study hard. He spoke to the Marquis de Marbois, the French minister in Philadel-

★

phia, about getting someone to teach Patsy French.

"I calculate the odds at about fourteen to one that Patsy will marry a blockhead," Jefferson said. And the Marquis laughed.

"My good sir," he replied, "a similar calculation has been made by every father in considering the matrimonial prospects of an attractive daughter."

But to be sure that Patsy didn't marry a blockhead, Jefferson wrote her a great number of letters and in one of them set out the schedule she should follow every day. It went like this:

From eight to ten each morning she was to practice music. From ten to one she was to dance one day and draw the next. From one to two she was to draw on the day she danced and presumably dance on the day she drew. From three to four she was to read French and from four to five she was to practice her music again and from five to bedtime she was to read English and practice writing.

When Patsy got this letter she sighed and shook her head. It was very hard being the daughter of Tom Jefferson. There was no time allowed for breakfast, lunch or dinner, or going for a walk, or playing, or coaxing her governess into taking her shopping. In fact there was no time at all for living, only time for working.

She did not follow the schedule. She was staying with Mrs. Thomas Hopkinson, mother of Francis Hopkinson, who was a friend of Jefferson. The good lady was sixty-five years of age and no match for Patsy. Mrs. Trist, a family friend, saw Patsy a few times and wrote to Jefferson saying that she was "very hearty" and hinting that she wasn't too particular about her clothes. Furthermore her drawing teacher, a Frenchman, was having trouble getting Patsy to draw the cubes and cylinders and spheres which were the basis of art instruction in those days.

Jefferson wrote his daughter on all these subjects. He told her she must be tidy and clean in her dress and never wear anything that was soiled. He could write with ease about the rights of man but lecturing his daughter on the charms of women made him awkward.

"Some ladies think they may, under the privileges of deshabille, be loose and negligent in their dress in the morning," he wrote, "but be you from the moment you rise till you go to bed as cleanly and properly dressed as at the hour of dinner or tea. . . . I hope therefore the moment you rise from bed your first work will be to dress yourself in such style as you may be seen by any gentleman without his being able to discover a pin amiss, or any other circumstance of neatness wanting."

He concluded his letter by writing, "If you love me then, strive to be good under every situation and to all living creatures. . . ."

To free the slaves, to establish a true democracy in the United States, to breed new plants and improve

★

the agriculture of the nation, to study the stars, to provide for the expansion of America to the coast of the Pacific and to bring up three daughters—these were the tasks of Thomas Jefferson. The last he sometimes found the most difficult.

11

In the colonial days in Virginia, tobacco had been money. A man could pay for a horse or the services of a doctor or for the support of his church in hogsheads of golden Virginia tobacco. There was always a shortage of real money in the colonies. English money had a habit of getting back to England and indeed many of the planters and traders of colonial days carried on their business by barter and credit. They shipped their goods to English merchants who shipped them goods in return or entered a credit of a certain value for them in their books.

The colonies of course could not mint coins or issue money of their own. Spanish dollars flowed in to mix with English pounds to make up the currency shortage and Tom Jefferson, journeying from Virginia to Philadelphia, paid his way from a purse which contained

English pounds and shillings, Spanish dollars, Dutch guilders and French louis d'or.

With the outbreak of the Revolution, the confused currency situation became impossible. All trade with England had ceased, credits dried up, bills went unpaid and many a soldier fought through the war without receiving any regular payment out of which to support his family.

With the coming of peace, it was essential to establish a currency for the United States of America. The Continental Congress had appointed a committee in 1776 to establish relative values of the different kinds of coins in circulation in the thirteen colonies. Three weeks after the adoption of the Declaration of Independence, Thomas Jefferson had been added to that committee which was led by Robert Morris, one of the wealthiest of Philadelphia's merchants.

Robert Morris was so well known in France and in England as a reliable businessman that his word alone was worth a credit of thousands of pounds. During the Revolutionary War he pledged his word to obtain arms, gunpowder and clothing for the Continental soldiers time and time again. Where French merchants might be unwilling to lend money to the United States of America, they would lend it to Robert Morris. He emerged from the war ruined—his whole trade gone, his ships sunk, his warehouses empty and in ruins. At one time he was imprisoned for debt. George Washington visited him in a debtor's prison to console him and promise him all the help he could to straighten his affairs.

This was the man then who, with Tom Jefferson and others, tackled the maze of American currency. Morris wanted to establish a currency based on a decimal system and Jefferson heartily supported him. The early report the Morris committee turned in to the Continental Congress was put aside. In 1782, however, the problem arose again and the Congress, in hiding from soldiers who had been paid with printing press money, asked Morris and Jefferson once more to look into the question. Morris drew up an elaborate statement in which he proposed the establishing of a unit of money based on the amount of pure silver in a penny. This unit would be 1/1440 part of a Spanish dollar or 1/1600 of the Crown sterling.

When Jefferson saw this his head was in a whirl. He got pen and paper and worked out the price of a loaf of bread at seventy-two of Morris' units; the price of a horse could not be expressed without using six figures. "Heavens," he said to Morris, "pity the poor farmer buying a bullock and selling a load of hay. He would be two weeks trying to find whether he had made a profit or a loss."

"See what *you* can do," said Morris. "The essential thing is to find a basic unit which will not disrupt whatever currency we have now."

Jefferson asked for a copy of Morris' plan, but those to whom they had been sent had put their copies aside

★

as too muddling for their brains and all were lost. Tom Jefferson took out his writing desk and started to do some figuring.

He decided a bigger unit was needed and hit upon the dollar. One-tenth of the dollar was to be called a dime, and one-hundredth part of a dollar would be a penny. He put his ideas together in a paper which he entitled "Notes on the Establishment of a Money Unit and of a Coinage for the United States." Robert Morris liked his plan but suggested some changes which Jefferson did not like. Jefferson printed his notes and circulated them to all the members of the Congress. They were finally agreed on and thus was brought into being the simple and efficient American currency which we use today.

On May 7, 1784, a great change occurred in Tom Jefferson's life. In the morning a letter arrived from Benjamin Franklin in Paris saying that John Jay, one of the commissioners appointed to negotiate the peace with England which had now been concluded, was returning to the United States. The news had hardly arrived before the members of the Congress decided they must send someone else to France to join John Adams and Benjamin Franklin in negotiating treaties of commerce with the European powers. Tom Jefferson was elected for this mission.

Jefferson was delighted. He had twice been deprived of an opportunity of going to France and now he was at last to have his chance. The Congress was still at Annapolis when he received this appointment; he immediately started paying his bills and writing letters to his friends, saying that he was to leave for Europe. He arrived in Philadelphia, went immediately to Patsy and told her that they were to go to Paris together.

"*Magnifique, Papa,*" cried Patsy, thus assuring her father at one and the same time that she had been studying her French and was delighted at the prospect of going to France.

Jefferson, to celebrate, took her to a play that night and a little later to see a balloon ascension. Balloons were all the rage in Philadelphia. In France, a year before, Joseph and Jacques Montgolfier had sent a hot-air balloon up a great distance and it had come down one and a half miles from its launching site. Every man of learning in America had details of this first ascension of a balloon from friends in France.

Experiments with balloons were started immediately in Philadelphia and Jefferson had received a letter from the Chevalier Luzerne describing how a balloon had gone up three hundred feet with a man aboard and had come down six miles away after a flight of twenty minutes.

Jefferson's friend, Francis Hopkinson, was experimenting with balloons made of paper. One was sent up from the garden of the Minister of Holland and another from the garden of Robert Morris. Jefferson had

★

141

to see such a marvel and he took Patsy with him and paid fifteen shillings for the privilege. He watched three balloons rise, the largest of them eight feet in diameter. It went up three hundred feet. He dashed off to see his friend James Monroe to tell him all about it and immediately started to study aeronautics.

"These balloons or something like them will change the world," Jefferson told Hopkinson. "For one thing fortresses can be destroyed by them and fleets of ships too, unless they can find some way of defending themselves from attacks from the air. More than that, inland countries will now be able to ship their goods by air and I believe the day will come when merchandise and people will travel from country to country on the wind. Mark what I say. We shall one day soar sublime above the clouds." He wished for a balloon himself and reckoned that if he had one he would be able to get from Philadelphia to Monticello in five hours instead of ten days.

Packing for France and making a last tour of Philadelphia's shops, Jefferson spotted outside the door of a hatter's shop a large panther's skin. In he went, determined to buy it.

"Whatever do you want with that, Papa?" Patsy asked for she felt, being the woman of the family, that she should keep an eye on her father's spending.

"I'm going to take it to Monsieur Buffon in Paris," said Tom Jefferson. "He says that there are no panthers in America but only cougars. I am going to prove

★
142

him wrong." The panther's skin cost Jefferson sixteen dollars.

"That's rather a lot of money just to prove the gentleman is wrong," said Patsy.

"In establishing truth," replied her father, "money is no consideration at all." He made one further payment before leaving America, giving seventeen pounds ten shillings to Francis Hopkinson to give to an artist in return for a portrait of George Washington. He took the portrait with him to Paris.

Jefferson was determined to see as much of America as he could before leaving for Europe. He had visited only Virginia, Maryland and Pennsylvania and decided he must certainly see the New England states and visit New York.

New York was as much of a fascination for him as it is for a tourist today. He couldn't resist the shops and spent six days in the city buying books and maps and sets of chessmen and a hat, until Patsy wondered how they were going to get all that luggage over to France.

Jefferson wouldn't leave without calling on Ezra Stiles, the president of Yale College. Stiles pumped him for all the information he could get about Virginia and particularly about the College of William and Mary at Williamsburg whose curriculum Jefferson had done a great deal to reform. Stiles was horrified to learn that a student did not have to know any Latin or Greek to get into William and Mary. Yale required such knowledge. He was excited when Jefferson told

★

him of the huge bones which had been recently dug up in Ohio. Jefferson himself owned a thigh bone three feet long and a tooth that weighed sixteen pounds.

Indeed Jefferson's interest in these huge bones was soon to gain for him the nickname of "Mastodon Tom." From New York Jefferson went to Hartford, Norwich, New London, Newport, Providence and Boston. Everywhere he discussed local government, the price of labor, the state of shipbuilding and fishing, exports and imports, determined that when he arrived in France he could speak with authority about his country. Finally he sailed on the ship *Ceres* from Boston on July 5. But before he went aboard, he bought some apples and oranges and to these purchases Patsy raised no objection.

Just before dawn the ship got underway. Tall Tom Jefferson and his little daughter Patsy stood at the stern watching the topsails being set, the anchors weighed, braces and sheets trimmed. The *Ceres* glided out in the morning wind and when the sun was up Boston was a toy town of tiny houses peeping over the horizon.

"I'm lonely," said Patsy suddenly, taking her father's hand.

"So am I," said Thomas Jefferson and put an arm around his daughter's shoulder to comfort her.

☆

12

When republican Thomas Jefferson sailed for Europe, two powerful kings were passing through a critical period of their reigns. King George III of England, a man whom Jefferson all his life thought of as a tyrant, was thinking of abdicating his throne. King Louis XVI of France had discharged his brilliant advisor Necker and in effect handed over his powers to his queen Marie Antoinette, who was gay and frivolous and empty-headed. He remained king but was ruled by his queen and her self-seeking advisors.

King George III was a simple stubborn man whom his subjects liked and called "Farmer George." He delighted to go about the countryside in a plain coach and talk over a gate with any farmer he met on the weather and the condition of the crops. He loved his queen and his children and with the loss of the colonies believed he had failed his country. And so he drafted a speech to be presented to Parliament announcing his decision to resign the throne. His ministers persuaded him not to resign.

George's decision not to resign was followed by so many troubles that he was finally driven mad. Louis' decision to leave more and more of his affairs in the hands of his queen resulted in his being beheaded.

But these two events were still some years in the future, undreamed of when Thomas Jefferson and his daughter Patsy, then twelve years of age, arrived in France after a very pleasant journey across the Atlantic. Their ship had been becalmed for two days off the Newfoundland banks. With sunny weather and no wind, Tom Jefferson and Patsy joined the passengers and crew in fishing for cod. They got plenty of them, so many indeed that they ate only the best parts of the fish and threw the rest overboard for there was no salt with which to preserve them.

The ship went first to Portsmouth, England, where they rested a week so Patsy could get over the effects of the voyage. Then they went to Paris where Jefferson got rooms in the Hotel d'Orleans while he looked for a house. The house he finally obtained was one of the finest in Paris; it belonged to the Count de L'Avongeac. It had extensive gardens and a court and a great number of rooms and it was soon thronged with the nobility of France, who came to pay their respects to the writer of the Declaration of Independence.

The French nobility were amazed at the intelligence

of the Americans. First there was Franklin, one of the great natural scientists of his day. Then John Adams, whose knowledge of law was second to no man's and who could carry on a conversation in French or Latin or Greek. And now here was Jefferson, master of half a dozen languages, expert on music, painting, architecture, agriculture, law, botany, geology and indeed on any subject to which the conversation might turn. What kind of people was this nation producing? they wondered. Lafayette, back in France, tried to explain the Americans to his countrymen. They were a new kind of man, he said, who called no one master and regarded freedom as the most precious possession a man could obtain.

Some of the French were a little jealous of these talented Americans, among them the Abbé Raynal. The *abbé's* favorite theory was that both animals and men degenerated in America. They tended to grow shorter and shorter with each generation and their minds became poorer and poorer.

Ben Franklin kept his house at Passy in the suburbs of Paris and one day invited a company to dinner, half Americans and half Frenchmen. The *abbé* was among the Frenchmen. The Americans were seated on one side of the table and the French on the other.

During the dinner the *abbé* could not resist bringing up his theory about the degeneracy of men and beasts in America. Wise old Ben Franklin listened to him carefully but with a twinkle in his eye.

"*Monsieur l'abbé,*" he said, "let us put your theory to

the test. Here we have one half Americans, one half Frenchmen and, by good fortune for our experiment, they are seated on opposite sides of the table. If all will stand up, we will soon see whether the Americans have degenerated." The whole company arose. Among the Americans there were three men who were over six feet tall. None of the Frenchmen topped five feet ten inches and the *abbé* himself was very short.

"Well," said the *abbé*, "there are exceptions to every rule."

"Monsieur," said Franklin, "in America, I assure you, exceptions are the rule."

Jefferson was delighted to be meeting Ben Franklin again and spent a great deal of time with the wise elderly philosopher who, eight short years before, had sat beside him consoling him while the Congress went over every word of the Declaration of Independence. Franklin, Jefferson knew, never tried to teach anything directly. He got all his messages over by little anecdotes and Jefferson listened carefully while the doctor told him humorous tales of the people of Paris and the French Court.

"You will perhaps meet," said Dr. Franklin, "a certain Count Falkenstein. He is often here at my house. Never make the mistake of calling him sire."

"Why should I give him such a title?" asked Jefferson.

"It is his proper title," said Franklin. "He is actually the Emperor Joseph II of Austria."

★

"And why does he come to Paris as Count Falkenstein?" asked Jefferson.

"Even kings get tired of being kings," said Franklin. "He has done a great deal to free the people of his country from serfdom but he makes the mistake that all kings tend to make—he thinks *he* is the law."

Franklin and Abigail Adams, wife of John Adams, schooled Jefferson in the ways of the French Court. He learned fast and observed the curious customs of the Court, but he never agreed with them and was horrified at the condition of the mass of the French people who lived in terrible poverty.

He learned to carry, when visiting a French nobleman, a very small hat. Franklin explained to him that he was never to put this on. It was to be held in the crook of the left arm. He was not to sit down in a French salon but to engage in conversation with one or two others while standing or walking briskly up and down the drawing room—always with the little hat in the crook of his arm.

This standing about and walking up and down of the men annoyed the sprightly Abigail Adams. It made such a confusion she found it hard to gossip and she liked gossip. Furthermore, the men often stood or passed between the ladies and the fireplace, cutting them off from the heat.

"If only they'd sit down decently around the fire and have a dish of tea, I'd enjoy these entertainments much more, Mr. Jefferson," she told him.

★

"If only I could put my hat down, so would I," said Tom Jefferson. Abigail Adams liked Tom Jefferson as much as her husband John did and wrote to her sister that he was "one of the choice ones of the earth."

Jefferson found it almost impossible to work in his fine house in Paris. There were callers at all hours of the day and they stayed until late in the evening. He had noted in his walks around the town a Carthusian monastery on Mount Calvary. He discovered that he could rent a room there for a small fee. He rented such a room and had with it the use of the gardens. The monks were forbidden to talk except when necessary and so a serene silence prevailed through the gardens and the monastery itself.

It was here that Thomas Jefferson went when he had serious work to do and wanted to get away from his visitors. He became friendly with the monks and even envied their life of devotion and meditation. He invited several of them to visit him in his fine townhouse and the abbot became so fond of him that he presented him with an ivory broom which had been made by one of the monks.

Lafayette was the one to whom all the Americans turned when they needed instructions in the etiquette of the French Court itself.

"You must learn about knocking on doors," Lafayette told Jefferson before his first visit to the palace of Versailles. "Or rather you must learn about *not* knocking on doors. At the Court it is the height of bad manners to knock on a door. You must scratch on it with your fingernail."

"Any particular fingernail?" asked Jefferson with a smile.

"Oh yes," said Lafayette, "that of the little finger of the left hand which should grow long for the purpose."

"You're joking," cried Jefferson.

"I'm deadly serious," said Lafayette. "You will be judged on these matters. There are other refinements too. When you make your first call on any of the great houses around the town, you do not scratch on the door, you knock."

"Excellent," said Jefferson. "I knock the first time and scratch afterwards."

"Not at all," said Lafayette. "The scratching is reserved for Versailles. The second time you call on a nobleman you give one blow of the knocker. No more. Two is regarded as outrageous bad manners. And you must learn how to behave in the presence of the King's dinner. You may be at Versailles when it is brought through the corridors. You must immediately bow low, sweeping the ground with your hat and murmur reverently, '*La viande du Roi?*' (The King's food?).

"You already know that you must stand in the presence of the King," Lafayette continued, "but please bear in mind that you must also stand in the presence of the King's messenger, or the messenger of any man whose rank is higher than yours."

Jefferson marveled at the ceremony that surrounded

the King of France. He found Louis XVI a good-natured and amiable man, but weak and utterly unaware of the condition in which his subjects lived. Louis liked to hunt and regarded that day lost on which he had not shot something. He also liked making locks, but he didn't like reading or anything that called for mental work.

He was awakened every morning at eight by a curious procession of servants. The first of these were the royal faggot bearers who came in to light the King's fire in winter. They were followed by the King's watchmaker who came in to wind the King's watch. Then came the royal wigmaker and from a huge assortment of wigs—walking wigs, sitting wigs, hunting wigs, council wigs and thinking wigs—he selected two, one to be worn while the King was dressing, the other while he had his breakfast.

At this point the King was not yet out of bed. He was awakened on the stroke of eight by his valet and through the huge palace of Versailles the exciting whisper spread, "The King is awake." The courtiers had to wait to see the King while the King's physician and the King's surgeon and the King's nurse came in to see if the Sovereign was well.

The two doctors rubbed him down and changed his shirt for him. And when the King was at last clad in a long shirt, the Grand Chamberlain opened the doors of the anteroom and in bustled the courtiers, their silks rustling like corn in the wind, all pretending the greatest eagerness to get a glimpse of their newly awakened sovereign which would support them through their day ahead.

The courtiers were soon put out while the King said a few prayers. But they were readmitted to watch him put on his dressing gown and wig and later a larger throng entered to watch the King put on his trousers. They always commented on how cleverly he managed this.

So the whole ceremony of the King's dressing and the King's breakfast went on. He washed his face in water mixed with spirits of wine and shaved every other day for shaving was too painful to be undertaken daily.

All this ceremony disgusted Jefferson to the soul. That any human being should be attended as a god horrified him, and his dislike of kings was intensified by his years in Paris during which time he was compelled to pay frequent visits to Versailles.

He was more disgusted when he contrasted the shallowness, elegance and astonishing waste at the King's Court with the grinding poverty of the people of Paris and France generally.

The people lived in tottering hovels on which no building had been done in a century or more. Some of the houses they occupied, if they could be called houses, were windowless and the roofs consisted of any kind of rubbish that could be put up to keep out the weather.

Sewage flowed down the streets in an odious glittering stream, horrid with offal and the corpses of cats and dogs. Chamberpots were emptied with impunity from upper windows with a cry of "*Garde-toi*" (watch yourself) to warn anyone who might be passing below. Some of the streets were paved with cobblestones, but the wretched people had dug up the cobbles in many places to try to repair the hovels they lived in.

The resulting potholes broke wheels and axles of carts and carriages that rumbled over them. Sewage water collected in these holes and little children, thin as sticks, played in these foul pools, in rags which bore not the slightest resemblance to clothing. They were called "*sans culotte*"—"people without trousers"— and the description was apt. These wretches, who rarely ate a full meal and who drank putrid water or worse wine, together with their brothers in the countryside supported with their taxes the luxury of the Court and of the nobility.

Jefferson was not long in Paris before he wrote a letter to Mrs. Trist in Philadelphia, who had helped take care of Patsy. "Of twenty million people supposed to be in France," he said, "I am of the opinion there are nineteen millions more wretched, more accursed in every circumstance of human existence, than the most conspicuously wretched individual of the whole United States."

He knew that such conditions could not continue; that human nature would not tolerate them. So did his friends among the nobility. These same nobles, whose own subjects were so wretched, had heartily supported the American Revolution against England's rule. To be sure, as Jefferson knew, much of their support came from France's centuries-long enmity toward England. But some of it came from a genuine love of liberty and many of them were deeply concerned about the condition of their own people.

But what was to be done to alter matters? That was the great question. In their perplexity the French intellectuals naturally turned to Jefferson and to Franklin and John Adams, who had been foremost in producing the American Revolution. But all three were ministers in a foreign country where they dared not interfere with internal affairs. They had to be careful of what they said.

Jefferson advised working for little gains, little improvements in government which, added year after year, would finally result in the liberation of the French people. But the people of France had before them the glittering and astonishing success of the American Revolution. The intelligentsia and the nobility might be prepared to take Jefferson's advice and slowly remake their government. The starving people of Paris and the French countryside were not. Jefferson noted something curious about them. When he stopped to ask a man his name, he would reply, "Jacques."

"And your friend?"

"Jacques."

★
155

"And this man here?"

"Jacques."

"They are all Jacques," said Jefferson to Lafayette later.

"Yes," replied the young nobleman grimly. "A common name and a common cause."

☆

13

Ben Franklin, when Jefferson arrived in Paris, was not well. John Adams had been in Holland and returned to France. Franklin wanted to return to his homeland although he had some doubts about leaving John Adams as Minister to France, for Adams distrusted the French who in return were not warm to him. But before Franklin could leave, the treaty of commerce, for which Jefferson had been sent to France, had to be negotiated, not merely with France but with all European nations who could be persuaded to sign it.

The treaty, drafted by the Congress, contained many of Jefferson's ideas on international trade. He believed that trade should be free—each country selling to the other, without import taxes, whatever it best produced. But world economy was too complicated for such an arrangement and regulation of trade by taxing imports was one of the weapons of government. Jefferson maintained that the United States should admit freely into its own country the goods of any nation which accepted American imports freely. If there were import taxes, they should be adjusted so that America taxed the goods of a particular nation in proportion as that nation taxed American goods.

Many American and British merchants had suffered heavy losses at the outbreak of the Revolutionary War by the seizure of their assets. Jefferson proposed that in the case of war merchants should have a period of several months in which to wind up their affairs without their goods being seized. He clearly saw that the threat of seizure in the case of war prevented the development of trade. He also wanted the nations to agree that unarmed ships should be free from capture by nations which were at war.

But none of the nations of Europe was interested in such a liberal treaty. Only Frederick the Great of Prussia signed the treaty and he had no navy and very little trade with the United States. One of the difficulties of negotiating a treaty with France was that the various American states had their own envoys in France at the same time trying to negotiate separate little agreements which would benefit themselves. The states were just not able to accept the idea of a federal government. They were prepared to support a central government, provided it kept its hands off what they regarded as their business. And shipping rum from

Massachuestts to France was something that Massachusetts looked on as its own affair.

In the spring of 1785, Benjamin Franklin at last secured the consent of the Congress for his return to America. Tom Jefferson was notified that he was to take over as Minister to France and was presented in this capacity to the Count of Vergennes, the French Minister of State. "You are to replace Monsieur Franklin?" the Count asked.

"I am to succeed him," replied Jefferson. "No one can replace him."

Before Franklin left, Jefferson heard that the members of the important Committee of States at home which he had proposed had come to loggerheads, split into two parties, quarreled violently and finally abandoned their duty. The committee had been set up to carry on the functions of the government while the Congress was not in session.

Jefferson was very disturbed that such a body, with such an important function, should abandon its work, leaving the United States without any tangible government. He spoke with Franklin on the matter and said, "What is it about men that makes them always divide into parties and quarrel with each other instead of working together?"

"My good sir," said Franklin, "it is human nature. Let me tell you a story. You are aware of the Eddystone lighthouse in the English Channel? It is manned by two men who take up their duties in the autumn and are not visited by any boat from the shore until the spring.

"One spring when the boat called at the Eddystone light with fresh supplies for the keepers, the boatman was met by one of them and asked, 'How goes it, friend?'

" 'Very well.'

" 'How is your companion?'

" 'I do not know.'

" 'Don't know? Is he not here?'

" 'I can't tell.'

" 'Have you not seen him today?'

" 'No.'

" 'When did you last see him?'

" 'Not since last fall.'

" 'You have killed him?'

" 'Not I.'

"They were about to arrest the man, concluding that he had certainly murdered the other keeper. But he told them to go upstairs and look for themselves. They went up and found the other man alive. The two had quarreled soon after being left on the lighthouse and had divided into two parties assigning the cares below to one and the cares above to the other. That, my friend," concluded Franklin, "is what happens with committees. A committee of two will produce two parties—sometimes three."

"Three?" cried Jefferson.

"When you have been a little while in France," replied Franklin, "you will see that it is perfectly possible for two Frenchmen to hold three points of view. They have a kind of genius for it."

The French reaction to the treaty of commerce, as given by the Count of Vergennes, was that France would prefer to negotiate piecemeal on different points and with that Jefferson, Franklin and Adams had to be content.

When Franklin returned to the United States, John Adams was appointed Minister to the Court of King George in England. When Adams had been in England a little while, he asked Jefferson to join him in London to try to obtain Britain's agreement to a treaty of commerce. Before Jefferson could leave, however, he had to provide for Patsy. He did not want to leave her in Paris with all its luxury unless she was in good hands, and could not take her to England for he did not expect to be away for more than a few weeks. So he left Patsy in a convent and visited her every day for two or three weeks until she had settled down there; then he left for England.

The two old friends cooled their heels in London for some days before being summoned to the palace so that Jefferson could be presented formally to King George III as an American minister.

Jefferson did not look forward to the meeting. In the Declaration of Independence he had denounced the King as a tyrant beyond the consideration of decent men. The world had read of this denunciation and Jefferson, who saw no reason to retract a word of it, expected that the King would show his resentment.

★
161

His expectation was fully realized. When the Lord Chamberlain, before the glittering court, called out, "Thomas Jefferson, Esquire, Envoy of the United States of America," and Jefferson advanced toward the King as protocol demanded, George deliberately turned his back on him.

Taking their cue from their sovereign, the courtiers left the two Americans severely alone. It was quite plain that no treaty of commerce was likely to be approved in such an atmosphere.

Jefferson was thoroughly outraged by the King's behavior. His feelings were not soothed by a pompous general who told John Adams and him that there was no sense in trying to get Britain to admit the United States as part of the British Dominions again.

"We will have nothing more to do with you, sirs," said the general.

"Excellent," replied Jefferson drily, "it appears we have not revolted in vain."

Snubbed by the court, Adams and Jefferson decided to take a tour of England and went off like a couple of schoolboys. Jefferson was especially delighted with the magnificent English gardens and begged for seeds of exotic plants to send back to America.

They visited all the historic places: Westminster Abbey, Oxford University, Shakespeare's cottage and many famous English battlefields. One of these battlefields was Worcester where Oliver Cromwell's army had routed the forces of King Charles II in the English Civil War.

★

A few English farm laborers and others gathered around to look at the two Americans, and Adams, moved by the battlefield on which Englishmen had themselves struck a blow at a tyrannous king, made a little speech to them about their revolution, saying they stood on hallowed ground. They received his speech in silence though Adams, who was inclined to vanity, thought he had made a very fine impression upon them.

Wherever they went, Jefferson took a sketchbook and a supply of ready money with him. At Kew near London he saw an Archimedes screw being used to pump water. He made a quick sketch of it to send to America.

He was shown a steam-run mill and soon understood all the details of its operation. He wrote to Charles Thomson, then secretary of the Congress, that using steam, a peck and a half of coal would perform as much work as a horse. America, he pointed out, had an abundance of coal and such steam mills would greatly increase the output of her factories. He even suggested that steam engines put in boats would "lay open all the streams to navigation."

Jefferson's concept of an ambassador was that he should not merely deal with the ministers of other countries but should also take note of all the things other countries had which were lacking in America and might be useful.

He was an ambassador not merely of the United States Congress but of American farmers, merchants

★

and mechanics. He bought as always a huge quantity of material—a thermometer, a solar microscope, a globe telescope, a hydrometer, all the scientific instruments being produced in England but lacking in the United States. He shipped back to the United States hares, rabbits, pheasants, partridges and a score of various seeds all of which he thought might be useful in his own country. He filled notebook after notebook with his English discoveries and this was only the start of scores of notebooks he would fill on his tour through Europe.

Whatever was new was of interest to Thomas Jefferson, who at times astonished the people of England, France and Italy with his knowledge of their countries. He set, as it were, a style for millions of American tourists who were to follow him, always asking questions, always poking into shops and buildings, always buying whatever took his fancy.

Jefferson, unrestrained by Patsy, bought two hundred books to send to his friend James Madison. They were books on law, on ethics and on philosophy and greatly influenced Madison's work on the United States Constitution. He wrote innumerable letters to the presidents of Harvard, Yale, William and Mary and the College of Philadelphia on European university systems and methods of teaching, and on experiments to steer a manned balloon. He would go fifty miles to see the construction of a new bridge or a new lock on a canal. Europe was a treasure house for Tom Jefferson

★

and he intended to get the best of the treasures to send back to the United States.

The mission to England was a failure, diplomatically, and Jefferson returned to Paris. While walking around the city, he fell and broke his right wrist. It was set by a doctor but did not mend properly and he was compelled for many months to write with his left hand and to give up one pleasure which meant a great deal to him—playing the violin. However busy he was, he had always had time for daily practice and carried about with him a little kit, a special violin which could be slipped in the pocket of a frock coat and so carried easily.

His wrist continued to give him pain and Jefferson was advised to journey to the south of France for his health. Before going, however, he wanted his little daughter Polly, whom he had left with Mrs. Eppes, to join him. He missed her. But Polly was not a traveler like her father; she had settled down with Mrs. Eppes, fallen in love with her, and wanted her father to come back home.

Tom Jefferson had to use all his powers as a diplomat to get Polly to leave Philadelphia and join him in Paris. He promised her "as many dolls and playthings as you want" and, in the same letter, trying his best to groom her into a young lady, told her "never tell stories, never beg for anything, mind your books . . . remember not to go out without your bonnet because it will make you very ugly."

★

Polly wasn't impressed with the offer of dolls in Paris. She wanted her father and her sister back in Philadelphia and she wrote one of the shortest letters Tom Jefferson ever received in his life. It read, "Dear Papa, I want to see you and sister Patsy but you must come to Uncle Eppes's house. Polly Jefferson."

There were many difficulties in getting Polly Jefferson to France. Ships sailed infrequently and Jefferson had to be sure that his little daughter sailed on a ship which belonged to a country paying tribute to the Barbary pirates. If she sailed on any other, and the ship were taken by the pirates, Polly would be sold into slavery.

Over and above this, Jefferson insisted that Polly must not come on a ship that was more than four or five years old. On the other hand it must be a vessel that had made at least one transatlantic crossing. With his usual care, he had looked into the figures of ships lost at sea and found that most were lost on their maiden voyage or when they were five years old.

Then there was the problem of getting an adult to accompany Polly across the Atlantic. Whoever was chosen should have had smallpox so the disease would not be communicated to Polly. Polly had been vaccinated but Jefferson was taking no chances. Every time he thought of his little daughter, his heart was wrenched; Patsy looked like him, but Polly was tiny and pretty like her mother.

It was not until the summer of 1787 that Polly finally

★

reached Europe. It took a plot to get her on board the ship. Mrs. Eppes took Polly to the ship with her own two children. They stayed aboard for a day or two and then while Polly was asleep her cousins went ashore and she woke up to find the ship at sea.

Polly was taken to England and Jefferson sent a trusted servant, Petit, to London for her. He could not leave France himself. Polly had been met in London by John Adams' wife Abigail. It wasn't long before Polly was as in love with Abigail Adams as she had been with her aunt Mrs. Eppes. In fact, on the way over to London she had become desperately attached to the ship's captain and Mrs. Adams had had a hard time persuading her to leave him.

John Adams' wife wrote to a friend in America about Polly: "I grew so fond of her and she was so much attached to me that when Mr. Jefferson sent for her they were obliged to force the little creature away. She is but eight years old. She would sit sometimes and describe to me the parting with her aunt who brought her up, the obligation she was under to her, and the love she had for her little cousins till the tears would stream down her cheeks; and how I had been her friend and she loved me. Her Papa would break her heart by making her go again. She clung around me so that I could not help shedding a tear at parting with her."

Finally Polly arrived in Paris to meet her father and Patsy. She had of course become enormously attached

★

to the servant Petit who had brought her. She stared at her tall father and her elder sister and clung to Petit's hand.

"Mistress Polly," said the servant, "that's your papa."

She eyed her father gravely. "If you pick me up, I shall cry," she announced.

"If I don't, I shall cry," said Thomas Jefferson. So he picked her up and soon she was trotting all around Paris with him and her sister, being bought innumerable dolls and telling them both of all the people she loved and how sad she had been to part with them.

After a time she went to a convent and Patsy had to go with her every day until she became used to it. She was soon the favorite of the nuns in the convent and was reducing them to tears with her recitals of all the people she loved and how she had had to part with them all.

She wept when she left the convent, too.

14

In France, meanwhile, a storm was brewing which rustled through the provinces in fitful bursts, swept violently and then died away in the streets of Paris. It did not ruffle a leaf in the great park of Versailles where King Louis XVI lived in his exotic court troubled by only two questions: how to supply his queen Marie Antoinette with the endless money she required for her pleasures, and how to find the time to go hunting.

The storm and its causes was well known to Thomas Jefferson. He wrote letters to George Washington and to James Madison and his other friends in the United States, forecasting its probable results. He had made an extensive tour through France and had visited the highest and the lowest in the country. He saw that the storm had its origin in the intolerable difference between the highest and the lowest. A center of high pressure represented by the nobility was neighbor to a center of extreme low pressure represented by the peasants. Nothing but a hurricane could result unless these pressures were relieved.

Jefferson knew the King well and his Queen too. The King he found an honest, well-intentioned, weak man with a genuine love of his country and of his subjects. The Queen he found a beautiful, pleasure-loving, brilliant woman with a will and an ambition as clear and as hard as a diamond. The Queen ruled the King and, supported by the arrogant nobility, ruled the land.

She spent in one night's gambling enough to take care of the needs of a whole French province for a year. She regarded it as her right to spend so extravagantly. Jefferson was constantly consulted by his friends, including Lafayette and the Duke of Orleans, on the need for a reform of the French government. He gave sane, sensible advice which was gratefully received. But no sanity could prevail against the will and extravagance of Marie Antoinette.

The finances of France, through the lavishness of the Court, got into such a state that more money had to be raised. The people, however, had been bled dry of money and the French nobility were united in the belief that taxes should be paid by peasants and not aristocrats.

Monsieur Necker, a Swiss financier of great sense who had previously been dismissed because he had fallen out of favor with Marie Antoinette, was recalled to save France from bankruptcy in the mounting crisis. The Queen hated him and so did the nobles, and whatever reforms he suggested were defeated by them.

An attempt was made to give the peasants and merchants a say in their government by establishing a third house of the French Parliament called the Third Estate. The First Estate was the Church and the Second was the nobility. But the greater part of the nobles and of the churchmen thought it beneath their dignity to meet in the presence of this Third Estate of common people.

Matters went rapidly from bad to worse. The Count of Vergennes, who had been the French Minister of Foreign Affairs, died and was replaced by the Count of Montmorin. The new Minister of Foreign Affairs received Jefferson and was soon confiding in him.

"The harvest has been very poor," he said. "Winter is coming and we have not produced enough wheat to feed the people with bread. Is it possible that our shortage can be filled from your country, Monsieur?"

"We may indeed have flour for export," replied Jefferson. "There is the difficulty of allowing it to be imported and sold in France."

"Leave that in my hands," said Montmorin. "We would be obliged to you for any flour you can supply and will pay well."

Jefferson had already negotiated a treaty whereby whale oil was to be admitted to the French market, but must be carried in either French or American vessels. He was acutely interested in employing American

★
171

seamen and American ships, for Britain at that time carried the greater part of the world's goods. The agreement concerning flour had a similar provision and in the months that followed over twenty thousand barrels of American flour were landed in the French Atlantic ports.

Montmorin's fears over a shortage of bread—which in France meant famine—were soon fulfilled. One day Tom Jefferson received a note from Lafayette inviting him to dinner. At the bottom of the note were the words, "Please bring your own bread." All invitations in Paris and throughout France soon contained the same request. However wealthy a man might be, he could get only a few ounces of bread a day for his household.

When Marie Antoinette saw the Paris mobs gathering outside the palace at Versailles, she inquired what they wanted.

"Bread, Your Majesty," she was told.

"Why don't they eat cake?" she asked, and the courtiers tittered. A nobleman, hearing of rioting taking place over the demand for bread, remarked that the peasants should eat grass if they were hungry. The news of this remark spread through Paris.

The winter of 1788-89 was the worst on record in France. Jefferson, consulting his thermometer religiously each day as he always did, recorded the temperature in Paris at fifty degrees below freezing on the Fahrenheit scale. The intense cold made it impossible for the shivering, starving, half-clad workmen of Paris to do any work. The rule was no work, no pay. But the government moved at last to help the people and ordered huge fires to be lit at all the crossroads of the city and bread to be given free to those who needed it.

Jefferson, walking through the streets—for he would go out in any weather—found thousands gathered around the street bonfires, chewing on gray bread frozen so hard they could scarcely bite it. He mingled with them and asked their names. Always the reply was the same. "My name is Jacques."

The bread famine was not relieved until midsummer. Meantime the storm of unrest grew more intense. A rumor that a big paper manufacturer in Paris was going to cut his wages threw the mob into such a rage that they attacked his house and his factory and destroyed everything in it. Soldiers were called out and fired on the mob and a hundred were killed before the crowd dispersed.

One of Jefferson's friends in Paris was Monsieur de Corny. He was a leader of a party which called itself the Patriots. Lafayette was another member. The object of the Patriots was not to depose the King but to reform the government. About the time of the American Revolution, Tom Paine had produced a pamphlet called *Common Sense* and this little book had united the country in its demand for freedom. Now Lafayette set about writing a pamphlet of his own for France which he called *A Declaration of the Rights of Man*. He consulted Jefferson over these rights and proposed to present them to the French Assembly when it met.

★
173

But the time had passed when France could be saved by meetings and declarations of rights. Even while the Assembly was in session the King, under the influence of selfish advisors, ordered a detachment of foreign troops to enter Paris "to keep order." Some of the French guards were arrested because they had called themselves "soldiers of the nation" rather than of the King.

The Paris mob stormed the prison, liberated the soldiers and sent a deputation to solicit a pardon for them. The King refused the pardon. Foreign troops were posted between Paris and Versailles for the King could not trust his own French troops.

Jefferson one day was visiting a friend and had to pass in his carriage by a square called the Place Louis XV. He saw a number of Swiss soldiers on duty in the road and a little farther on a hundred German cavalry.

He passed through these groups of soldiers and came upon a mob of people standing sullenly behind several large piles of stone. They let his carriage through without a word but as soon as he had gone by they started flinging stones at the German horsemen.

The cavalry charged. Jefferson got out of his carriage and saw the Paris mob fling such a shower of stones at the horses that the cavalrymen were driven back. The Swiss soldiers neither moved nor fired.

This attack on the troops was the signal for the general uprising in Paris. As Jefferson drove on to his house, he saw people breaking into armorers' shops

★

and into private houses searching for weapons. All night long Paris was a seething mass of people, grimly arming themselves. The next day they stormed the prison of St. Lazare, released all the prisoners, took all the arms they could find and took a great store of corn to the corn market.

The storm had broken at last.

St. Lazare had been taken by the Paris mob on July 13, 1789. On July 14, Jefferson's friend, Monsieur de Corny, who had put himself at the head of the armed people of Paris, went with five others to the Bastille to ask Monsieur de Launay, the governor, for arms. There was a huge crowd outside the ancient fortress which had never been successfully besieged.

De Corny raised a flag of truce and a flag of truce was raised on the walls of the Bastille. He went forward to ask the governor for arms but, as he did so, those in the Bastille opened fire, killing four people in the crowd.

There was one moment of horrified silence and then a shriek of rage and the mob hurled itself against the fortress. In a matter of minutes they were inside. They dragged the governor and the lieutenant governor out to the nearby Place de Grève where executions were held; they then cut off their heads.

Jefferson, watching from his window, saw a vast mob parading through the streets armed with bill-hooks, spears and pikes. And on two of the pikes were the heads of the governor and lieutenant governor of

★

the Bastille. A little later another head was paraded on a pike through the streets. The lips were stained green. It was the head of the nobleman who had told the starving peasants that if they were hungry they should eat grass. The mouth was stuffed with grass.

Jefferson, as United States Minister to France, could take no part in the French Revolution on one side or the other. But he well knew that the people of France had been inspired to their revolution by the American Revolution. Lafayette was part of the American Revolution and now was part of the French Revolution. Jefferson privately cautioned his friend to beware of excess.

"Lasting revolution bringing benefits to men is achieved by thought and not violence," he said.

"All will be over in a year," said Lafayette. "Then we will have in France the same justice, the same freedom, the same equality among men that you have in America."

They both believed this. Neither foresaw the mounting violence, the condemning to death of so many people that a special machine, the guillotine, had to be constructed to speed up the beheadings. Neither believed that both the King and the Queen of France would soon be beheaded.

Even before the bloody outbreak of the French Revolution, Jefferson had been hoping to return to America and Monticello. Work on his house was at a standstill while he was away. He was concerned about his plants and his slaves. He felt that he had done all he could in his country's service and began to need, after his travels, the rest he could only find at home.

The Constitution of the United States had now been ratified and George Washington elected the first President. Before this event Jefferson had written to Mr. John Jay, president of the Congress, asking to be allowed to return for five or six months to bring his daughters home and look after his own affairs.

He was beginning to be a little worried about Patsy. Patsy had now been in a convent for several years. She surprised him one day with a letter announcing her intention to become a nun and remain in a convent, devoting herself to religion for the rest of her days. Tom Jefferson, when he received this letter, was wise enough not to make any direct reply. Instead he visited the abbess at Patsy's convent, discussed the matter with her, and then took Patsy out of the convent for a few days to show her another kind of life.

He took her, in fact, to a brilliant ball at the King's palace at Versailles. And when Patsy found herself dancing with counts and viscounts and dukes in a palace where the crystal chandeliers seemed like a cascade of diamonds, she made no more mention of spending the rest of her life in a convent.

Polly was still the bright affectionate little girl, taking everyone into her heart. Her father sometimes wrote a dozen letters in a day and, to cut down on this work, had bought a copying machine in England so that one letter could be sent to half a dozen friends. Polly could not be brought to write a letter at all. She was always going to write one. She would get a pen and paper and seat herself very briskly at the writing table and tell her father that he must be quiet because she was going to write a letter. Then there would be a moment's silence and Polly would say, "Papa, I do not know what to say. You must help me." But Tom Jefferson resolutely refused to help her. So Polly never got any letters written.

Jefferson began to understand that his daughters needed a mother and sending them to a convent of kindly nuns in France was not the answer. He had promised his wife Martha, on her deathbed, that he would never marry again and indeed, although he was intellectually attracted to many women, he never loved anyone but Martha. The answer then was to take the girls back to America, to his sister, Mrs. Eppes, who loved them both.

Suddenly all roads seemed to lead to America and all roads in America to Monticello. He was homesick. When George Washington became President, Jefferson wrote to him in the spring of 1789. He congratulated Washington on his election, referred to his previous letter to Mr. Jay and begged to be allowed to come home. Washington replied, giving his permission.

Jefferson left with mixed feelings. He loved France.

★

He had as many friends in France as he had in the United States. He firmly believed that France was about to enter on a glorious future of freedom. He intended to return again to France some day.

But, for the present, he had to go back to Monticello. Something deep and strong was calling him there.

Anxious to return now that he had permission, Jefferson was delayed ten days at Le Havre before he could get a ship across the channel to England, from which he was to sail to the United States. He arrived at last at Cowes on the Isle of Wight only to face another ten days' delay because of contrary winds. He spent his time exploring the island and visiting places of interest, such as Carisbrook Castle where Charles I was kept a prisoner. Finally the wind turned fair and a fleet of thirty vessels—bound for America but detained at Cowes by adverse winds—set sail.

Jefferson's ship made a quick and pleasant voyage across the Atlantic to the Capes of the Chesapeake. When the vessel arrived offshore, however, a thick mist arose which entirely hid the coast. For three days the ship beat about and the mist still held. Finally the captain decided to sail in for the coast which he could not see. He explained his intentions to Jefferson as the most important passenger aboard.

"These mists are often the forerunners of a storm at this season of the year," the captain said. "If we lie here, the wind will pipe up and we are liable to be blown many miles out to sea and be another three

★

weeks or more reaching harbor. In these circumstances I am going to head in, hoping the mist will lift enough for me to see the land."

Patsy was now seventeen years of age, an attractive and stately young woman, and she greatly admired the captain's boldness. The other ships which had left England with them stayed where they were, but Jefferson's vessel clawed her way blindly into the wind, with a man standing in the main shrouds heaving a leadline to take soundings.

The wind increased and the bottom began to shoal. The captain decided to anchor, and during the night the ship lay in the mouth of the Capes of the Chesapeake anchored in a rising gale. By morning the mist had lifted and they found themselves well within sight of land. There was, however, a very strong head wind.

"I must keep my topsails flying to drive against this wind, Mr. Jefferson," the captain said. "But do not be alarmed if they carry away. It is a risk I must take if we are to get safely home."

Jefferson smiled. "I know little of navigation," he said, "but you and I are both old enough to recall a time when the whole nation, as it were, kept its topsails flying in the teeth of the gale and came safely through."

With the wind shrilling in the rigging, the ship heeled over, sending the water flying past her in a white scud as she clawed into the bay.

The ship had been no more than half an hour at this work when the main topsail sheets parted and in a

★

matter of minutes the big sail was reduced to a tattered rag streaming from the yardarm. But the sail had done its work and the ship was now deep inside the Cape.

Yet some evil fortune seemed determined to prevent Jefferson from reaching port. Suddenly a huge brig appeared out of the lowering storm and swept down on the ship running before the wind. It was impossible to alter course for the yards, sheets and braces could not be handled fast enough. The brig grew bigger and bigger until its bowsprit seemed about to thrust over the deck of Jefferson's ship. The helmsman had his wheel hard to port and this alone saved them. The brig's bowsprit tore through the backstays of the ship on which Jefferson was traveling—but a collision was avoided.

At last Jefferson and his daughters arrived at Norfolk, glad to get ashore and stretch their legs. Before leaving the ship Jefferson spoke to the captain, saying that he had in his cabin besides his own personal possessions many important state papers. He was anxious about their security.

"I will lock your cabin door myself, Mr. Jefferson," the captain said. "Do not be concerned. Everything will be safe."

But Tom Jefferson, Patsy and Polly were ashore only long enough to take breakfast at a tavern near the waterfront when they heard people shouting in the streets that there was a ship on fire in the harbor. Full of foreboding, Jefferson hurried to the waterfront. The

★

181

ship which he had just left was ablaze, tongues of flame licking up the rigging and masts. There was nothing he could do but stand there, berating himself for not bringing the important state papers ashore.

Volunteers from other vessels, however, came over to fight the fire and succeeded in putting it out. As soon as he could, Jefferson went aboard and the captain spotted him. "Everything is all right, Mr. Jefferson," he cried. "Your papers are safe. Your cabin is untouched."

He led him to the cabin and opened the smoldering door. Not a thing inside had been harmed though the heat was still intense. Indeed the temperature inside the cabin had been so high that the powder in a musket had burned, but had not exploded because it was not rammed tight. The Jeffersons' stateroom was the only one which had not been burned out.

Jefferson had written to his overseer at Monticello saying that he was returning and he now sent a further message that he would be home on December 23 to celebrate Christmas at Monticello.

The slaves at Monticello and at Shadwell, another of Jefferson's estates four miles distant, begged the overseer to be given the day off. They all gathered at Monticello awaiting the approach of Jefferson's carriage on the morning of December 23. When the carriage did not immediately appear, they walked from Monticello down the mountain to Shadwell. They were all in their very best clothes, men, women and children.

★

They reached Shadwell just as the carriage arrived there. They swarmed around it so that it was impossible for the horses to go through them. Some were laughing, some crying. They all tried to get to the carriage to get a glimpse of Jefferson and his daughters.

They unharnessed the horses and, seizing the shafts of the carriage, pulled Jefferson up the mountain to his home. When he got there, they lifted him up and carried him bodily up the steps to Monticello, laughing and singing, and held up thus, he could see over their heads the dark line of the Blue Ridge Mountains that he loved.

The trees were bare of leaves but the winter's sun, traveling west, filtered a silvery light over the tops of the mountains. Patsy remembered something she had told him on another homecoming many years before when she was a tiny girl.

"There is a dawn in the trees, Papa," she whispered to him.

"Yes," said Jefferson with tears in his eyes. "There *is* a dawn in the trees."

And so there was, for he was home again.

END OF THE SECOND VOLUME

★

PUBLISHER'S NOTE

Leonard Wibberley did not send a bibliography for *A Dawn in the Trees* before sailing in his yawl *Bahia* for Hawaii and points west. Therefore the publisher has included the following extract from the bibliography for *Young Man from the Piedmont*, Mr. Wibberley's first book in his multi-volume life of Thomas Jefferson.

"If you will go to your public library—and I hope you will—and look at the card index under JEFFERSON, THOMAS, you will find a highway of cards traveling off into the distance of the drawer, each one of them cataloguing a book about the man who was given the job of drafting the Declaration of Independence. There is then no need for me to include in this book a bibliography on Thomas Jefferson. Any library has lots of books on Jefferson in all his phases; philosopher, inventor, architect, agriculturalist, musician, traveler, diplomat, President of the United States; whatever the aspect of his career, there is a multitude of books on the subject.

"The best all-round book, essential to a knowledge of Jefferson and his times, is, in my opinion, *Origins of the American Revolution* by John C. Miller (Atlantic-Little, Brown). There isn't much of Jefferson in it; only a mention or two. But to understand Jefferson as anything but a pedant who, surprisingly, wrote the famous Declaration, it is essential to understand his times. *Origins of the American Revolution* is the best introduction to them.

"Jefferson in his later years wrote a brief autobiography,

★

but he was no Walpole. He did not write intimately about himself, and so his autobiography is only a summary of the main events of the first two thirds of his life. But coming from such a mind and hand it is well worth reading, and there are revealing little glimpses of Jefferson, the man, to be seen through the Augustan prose of the eighteenth century.

"Marie Gould Kimball's *Jefferson—The Road to Glory,* is a carefully researched volume on Jefferson's youth. It reads, I am sorry to say, a bit like a treatise for a college degree in many places. Yet it is a most valuable volume containing a mass of information on Jefferson's early years.

"Other books I found valuable were *Thomas Jefferson* by William Eleroy Curtis and *Life and Writings of Thomas Jefferson* by Samuel Eagle Forman. There are indeed a host of books on Jefferson; and I even found the neglected *Life and Times of Washington* by Washington Irving not only pleasant reading, but full of anecdotal detail which is the lifeblood of any book.

"I hope no one is going to take this book as one of learning. I have been at pains to be accurate and have not consciously put down any inaccuracy concerning Thomas Jefferson. This book is nonfiction fiction. Let my friends the librarians puzzle over the classification. For the reader, I hope only that he enjoys it."

Leonard Wibberley

Hermosa Beach,
California.

★

INDEX